100% Online STUDENT SUCCESS

ROXANNE DUVIVIER

D1517549

DELMAR
CENGAGE Learning™

Australia • Brazil • Japan • Korea • Mexico • Singapore • Spain • United Kingdom • United States

DELMAR
CENGAGE Learning™

100% Online Student Success
Roxanne DuVivier

Vice President, Career Education SBU:
Dawn Gerrain

Director of Learning Solutions: John Fedor

Acquisitions Editor: Martine Edwards

Managing Editor: Robert Serenka, Jr.

Associate Product Manager: Anne Orgren

Editorial Assistant: Michael Spring

Director of Production: Wendy Troeger

Production Manager: Mark Bernard

Content Project Manager: Mark Bernard

Art Director: David Arsenault

Technology Project Manager:
Sandy Charette

Director of Marketing: Wendy E. Mapstone

Channel Manager: Gerard Mcavey

Marketing Coordinator: Jonathan Sheehan

Cover Design: Suzanne Nelson

For product information and technology assistance, contact us at
Cengage Learning Customer & Sales Support, 1-800-354-9706

For permission to use material from this text or product,
submit all requests online at **cengage.com/permissions**
Further permissions questions can be emailed to
permissionrequest@cengage.com

Library of Congress Control Number: 2007941743

ISBN-13: 978-1-4283-3647-6

ISBN-10: 1-4283-3647-8

For more information, contact Cengage Learning,
5 Maxwell Drive,
Clifton Park, NY 12065
Or
find us on the World Wide Web at **http://www.cengage.com**

For permission to use material from this text or product, contact us by
Tel (800) 730-2214
Fax (800) 730-2215
www.cengage.com

Notice to the Reader

Publisher does not warrant or guarantee any of the products described herein or perform any independent analysis in connection with any of the product information contained herein. Publisher does not assume, and expressly disclaims, any obligation to obtain and include information other than that provided to it by the manufacturer.

The reader is notified that this text is an educational tool, not a practice book. Since the law is in constant change, no rule or statement of law in this book should be relied upon for any service to any client. The reader should always refer to standard legal sources for the current rule or law. If legal advice or other expert assistance is required, the services of the appropriate professional should be sought.

The publisher makes no representations or warranties of any kind, including but not limited to, the warranties of fitness for particular purpose or merchantability, nor are any such representations implied with respect to the material set forth herein, and the publisher takes no responsibility with respect to such material. The publisher shall not be liable for any special, consequential, or exemplary damages resulting, in whole or part, from the reader's use of, or reliance upon, this material.

Printed in United States of America
1 2 3 4 5 6 7 XXX 11 10 09 08 07

Table of Contents

3 TECHNICAL CONSIDERATIONS 36

4 **YOUR UNIQUENESS FACTOR** **60**

8 HEALTH CONSIDERATIONS FOR THE ONLINE STUDENT... 156

9 FINANCIAL CONSIDERATIONS 178

Find It Fast

Preface

CONGRATULATIONS!

Welcome to the world of online learning. Your enrollment in online learning says that you have made a decision to grow and develop as a person and professional. Your online learning experience will provide valuable knowledge and insights over the course of your lifetime. *100% Online Student Success* provides the tools to develop your professional and personal skills and to accomplish your goals.

HOW WILL THIS TEXT HELP YOU?

100% Online Student Success covers topics that are fundamental to professional success. The following are the main themes for the topics in the text. Take a look at these to get a general idea of the book and to see how each topic supports your academic success.

▶ **ELEMENTS OF SUCCESS IN ONLINE EDUCATION.** You will learn general skills needed for success in life and specific skills needed to achieve your goals in online education. The abilities to communicate and interact effectively, get organized, manage time, and handle technology are examples of success skills. Understanding the importance of these skills will prepare you for developing them further.

▶ **ADDRESSING BARRIERS TO ONLINE LEARNING.** You will learn how to address common deterrents faced by students pursuing higher education. By taking proactive and positive steps, you can remain focused and achieve your goals.

▶ **FINDING OUT ABOUT LEARNING STYLES AND ENVIRONMENTS.** Have you ever wondered how and where you learn best?

What is your learning style? Do you understand the impact your learning style and environment can have on your success in online learning? Knowing your learning style will help you choose the appropriate study activities from which you will learn best. You will explore your learning style and the activities and environment that support it.

▶ **ENHANCING CRITICAL LEARNING SKILLS.** You will learn strategies for improving core skills such as class participation and memorization. You will also learn how to get more out of reading and writing assignments, group work, lectures, and fieldwork.

▶ **DEVELOPING COMMUNICATION AND TECHNICAL SKILLS.** New technology and economic changes affect the job market of the future. You will learn ways to develop your communication and technical abilities, which are two skills employers value highly.

▶ **MANAGING YOUR HEALTH AND FINANCES.** Personal management skills such as taking care of your health and managing your finances are important components of success. You will explore how these elements affect your learning, and you will master techniques for managing them successfully.

HOW TO USE THIS BOOK

100% Online Student Success is written to actively involve you in developing positive and productive personal and professional skills. The following features will help guide you through the material and provide opportunities for you to practice what you've learned:

▶ **THE "BIG PICTURE."** The Big Picture, provided at the beginning of each chapter, is a kind of site map intended to give you an overview of chapter contents in relation to the other chapters in the text. As you read through the material, you are encouraged to recognize and consider the relationships among the various concepts and pieces of information you are learning.

▶ **LEARNING OBJECTIVES.** Learning objectives outline the information in each chapter. Use them to identify the important

THE BIG PICTURE

CHAPTER

10
9
8
7
6
5
4
3
2
1

points and to understand what you are supposed to learn. Also, use the learning objectives as a tool to measure what you have mastered and what you still need to work on. You are encouraged to expand on these objectives according to your goals and interests.

▶ **TOPIC SCENARIOS.** At the beginning of each chapter, a scenario demonstrates the application of chapter concepts to the real world. Use the questions following each scenario to stimulate your critical thinking and analytical skills. Discuss the questions with classmates. You are encouraged to think of your own ideas regarding how to apply concepts and raise additional questions.

▶ **REFLECTION QUESTIONS.** Reflection questions ask you to evaluate your personal development and encourage the development of thinking skills. This section is intended to increase your self-awareness and ability to understand your decisions and actions.

REFLECTION QUESTIONS

- How do you use critical thinking in your daily life? In school?
- How do you use creative thinking in your daily life? In school?

▶ **APPLY IT!.** After many sections of text, you will find activities that help you apply to real-life situations the concepts discussed in the section. Your instructor may assign these as part of the course requirements. If they are not formally assigned, it will be helpful to complete them for your own development. Three types of activities are available:

INDIVIDUAL ACTIVITIES are directed at your personal development.

GROUP ACTIVITIES typically include projects that are most successfully completed with the addition of several perspectives or broad research. A team effort adds to the success of these learning projects.

INTERNET ACTIVITIES are intended to help you further develop your online skills.

You may find it helpful to combine the activity types. For example, an individual project may require Internet research.

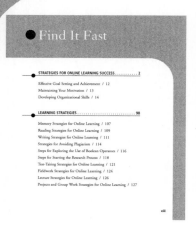

Some individual activities can be adapted to group activities, and vice versa. Use the activities as guides, and modify them in ways that best support your learning.

▶ **SUCCESS STEPS.** Success steps are included throughout the text and provide concise steps for achieving various goals. They are offered as a summary of each process. Details of each step are discussed fully in the body of the text. Are you looking for success steps to achieve a specific goal? Use the "Find It Fast" section in the front of the book to locate the steps you need.

▶ **LEARNING OBJECTIVES AND LEARNING OBJECTIVES REVISITED.** Chapter learning objectives, like those provided on course syllabi, outline what you should be learning from the chapter. The learning objectives should guide you to the main concepts of the chapter. Refer back to the learning objectives frequently, and pay attention to how chapter material adds to your knowledge related to each objective. Learning Objectives Revisited provides an opportunity for you to assess the effectiveness of your learning and to set goals to expand your knowledge in a given area. The Learning Objectives Revisited grid and instructions for its use are found at the end of each chapter. The example show here is taken from Chapter 1 of the *100% Online Student Success* textbook.

SUPPLEMENTARY MATERIALS

In addition to the textbook, the following supplemental materials are available:

▶ **STUDENT ONLINE COMPANION.** Textbook activities are supported by additional resources located in the Online Companion (OLC). OLC resources include quizzes, tips, tools, and Web resources. Access the OLC at http://www. delmarlearning.com/companions.

▶ **INSTRUCTOR ONLINE COMPANION.** Additional resources for instructors only are included on the Instructor Online Companion. These resources include PowerPoint presentations by chapter, lesson plans, chapter assessments, and assessment answer keys.

DEVELOPING YOUR ONLINE LEARNING SUCCESS PLAN

An excellent next-step resource that provides tools and strategies for success is *Your Online Learning Success Plan*. This online program is designed to increase your success by first asking you questions to determine your personality assessment. This reveals your advantages and disadvantages as an online learner and provides suggestions for increasing your success. You will develop an individualized plan where you commit to strategies that will keep you focused and motivated.

Your Online Learning Success Plan is a way to personalize and develop the strategies that are recommended in this book.

BEYOND ONLINE STUDENT SUCCESS

What are your goals for after you complete your online coursework? For most students, the typical goal is to become employed and achieve success in their field. Success begins with the skills you develop and practice in your online learning program. *100% Online Student Success* lays the foundation for the next two texts in the series of three books, *100% Job Search Success* and *100% Career Success*.

The professional and technical skills that you practice and develop in school become skills that are desirable to employers. *100% Job Search* Success expands on the skills that you have practiced by applying them to finding the job of your choice. The third book in the series, *100% Career Success*, takes you into the workplace and provides strategies for using your skills to add to your success as an employee.

The DuVivier "My E-Quity" Analysis

MY E-QUITY QUIZ

This quiz identifies strengths you have that will help you become an effective online learner. It also identifies other skills you need to acquire to ensure success in the online learning environment.

Answer each question as honestly as you can.

Decide whether the following statements are true of you always, sometimes, or never. Mark your answer in the correct box.

(Score as A - Always, S - Sometimes, N - Never)

LIST 1

My Traits

	A	S	N
1. I clearly understand my strengths and weaknesses.	A	S	N
2. I have a positive mental attitude. I see possibilities and I make them happen.	A	S	N
3. I have a network of people who know me and like me.	A	S	N
4. I know what the next steps are to get things done.	A	S	N
5. I have a good sense of timing. I know when to act and when to wait.	A	S	N
6. My learning style is a good fit for taking classes online.	A	S	N
7. I know what to say and when to say it. I am a skillful communicator.	A	S	N

LIST 2

My Skills – Academic Planning

	A	S	N
1. I have strong organizational skills. I make lists, keep files, and always know where things are.	A	S	N

2. I manage my time effectively.   A   S   N
   I am realistic about how long things take, and I plan accordingly.

3. When I set goals, they are practical and attainable.   A   S   N

4. I have a network of people who help me academically.   A   S   N

LIST 3

My Skills – Content Management

1. I learn a lot by reading assignments. I find purpose in   A   S   N
   my reading and can be quizzed about the facts I've read.

2. I am a strong writer. I outline my thoughts and express   A   S   N
   my ideas with well-cited source material.

3. I am skillful in memorizing facts and information and in   A   S   N
   demonstrating what I remember on tests.

4. I test well in any type of exam. I follow the rules, stay calm, A   S   N
   avoid distractions, and keep pace to finish on time.

5. I enjoy a good discussion. I make meaningful contributions.   A   S   N
   I respect the opinions of others and often learn from them.

6. I am a self starter. I can find field placement opportunities   A   S   N
   for myself and will manage the learning environment well.

7. I stay attentive while watching online lectures and video   A   S   N
   conferences. I know when to ask questions during the live feed
   and how best to review material afterwards.

8. I have strong project-management skills. I am comfortable as   A   S   N
   a team member or team leader. I set milestones to keep the
   project progressing to deadline.

LIST 4

My Behavior

1. I always am in attendance when I should be.   A   S   N

2. I actively involve myself in my work. I relate well and often   A   S   N
   to peers and communicate regularly with my teachers.

3. When I have a goal, I persist to goal completion.   A   S   N

LIST 5

My Technical Considerations

1. I have access to the equipment I need for online learning   A   S   N
   (computer, printer, modem, and mouse).

My Technical Skills

1. I have solid desktop computing skills.	A	S	N
2. I have strong online research skills.	A	S	N
3. I have access to the software packages I will need.	A	S	N
4. I can access the Internet.	A	S	N
5. I have access to technical support when I need it.	A	S	N
6. I have security systems in place to protect against loss/theft of my work.	A	S	N
7. I have an ergonomically designed office.	A	S	N

LIST 6

My Barriers – Health

1. My health is excellent. My family and I have no major health problems or concerns.	A	S	N
2. My financial health is excellent. I have the funds I need to go to college and stay there.	A	S	N
3. My personality is well suited to online learning. I am an independent, self motivated, and disciplined learner.	A	S	N

● E-QUIZ SCORING

MY TRAITS

1. Self understanding	Chapters 4, 5
2. Positive mental attitude	Chapter 1
3. Networking skill	Chapters 1, 2, 7
4. Next-step training	Chapter 1
5. Sense of timing	Chapter 1
6. Good communicator	Chapters 1, 2
7. Learning Style	Chapters 5, 6

MY SKILLS – ACADEMIC PLANNING

1. Organizational skills	Chapter 1
2. Time management	Chapters 1, 7

SCORING INTERPRETATION

ALWAYS   Congratulations! These are important skills to succeed in online learning, and they are part of your skill set. Use them to the fullest to attain success.

SOMETIMES   It looks like you have these important skills but don't always use them. Make a special effort to practice using these skills and apply them in your online classes. They will help you to do your best.

NEVER   As you work through the *100% Online Student Success* program, pay special attention to the highlighted sections. They focus on important online learning skills that you have yet to acquire. Make it a point to over-practice these sections until your new behavior becomes second nature.

About the Author

ROXANNE DuVIVIER has spent 30 years as a teacher, counselor, higher education consultant and college administrator. She has gained a national reputation in applying personality and learning theory to improve college student success.

Roxanne has won a number of awards for her work, including the 2005 Golden Lamp Award for her software product, "Your Strategic Future". Her latest web-based tool, "Your Online Learning Success Plan," was released in 2007.

Roxanne lives and works in southeastern Ohio and on the east end of Long Island in New York.

Acknowledgments

The author and publisher would like to thank the reviewers, whose feedback helped to shape the final book:

JoAnna Almasude, MFA
The Art Institute of Pittsburgh, Online Division, Pittsburgh, PA

Christina Bumgardner, M.S., Dean of Faculty,
Minnesota School of Business, Richfield, MN

Sherry Jones, M.T. (ASCP), PMST
Salt Lake City, UT

Nancy McGee, Ph.D.
Macomb Community College, Warren, MI

Susan Roudebush, M.S., Educational Consultant
Susan Roudebush Consulting, Ashland, OR

Vickie Saling, M.Ed., Director of Career Services
Heald College, Hayward, CA

Image copyright Sean Nel, 2009. Used under license from shutterstock.com

CHAPTER OUTLINE

1

Strategies for Online Learning Success

THE BIG PICTURE

LEARNING OBJECTIVES

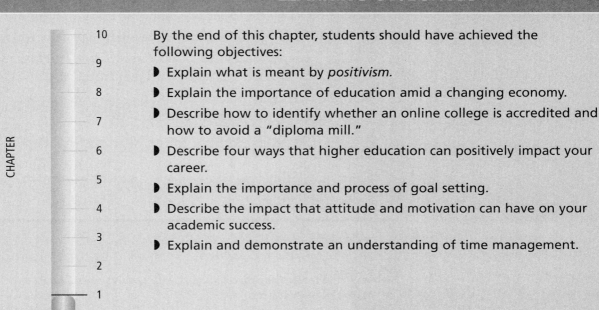

By the end of this chapter, students should have achieved the following objectives:

- Explain what is meant by *positivism.*
- Explain the importance of education amid a changing economy.
- Describe how to identify whether an online college is accredited and how to avoid a "diploma mill."
- Describe four ways that higher education can positively impact your career.
- Explain the importance and process of goal setting.
- Describe the impact that attitude and motivation can have on your academic success.
- Explain and demonstrate an understanding of time management.

CHAPTER

10
9
8
7
6
5
4
3
2
1

1

TOPIC SCENARIO

Nicole had been an average student, preferring to go with the flow and not stand out. She didn't finish her associate's degree in advertising because she was promoted to assistant manager at her retail job, and that meant increased hours. At first, she tried to take night classes to finish her degree but eventually concluded that she just couldn't make it work.

Recently, she has grown dissatisfied with doing the same things day in and day out. Her manager often catches her staring into space as she contemplates the different path her life could have taken or could still take. Through self-reflection, Nicole concluded that if she made some changes in her life, she could still get her degree!

On her lunch breaks, she began writing down a game plan. She knew that in the world of advertising, she would need to make her presence known, so she set a goal to meet more people. Her next goal was to research online advertising programs where she could transfer some of the credits she had already earned toward her degree. After she completed that goal, she would enroll in one or two classes as a trial. Nicole knew that she would have to manage her time better than she had been in the past, so she wrote down the goals and established dates for completion. She was on her way.

Based on Nicole's situation, answer the following questions:

▶ What potential roadblocks to success did Nicole's self-analysis reveal, and how did she plan to overcome them?

▶ To what means are you responsible for your own success at attaining a degree of higher education?

▶ What areas might you need to develop to become a better student?

▶ How can setting and writing down goals help you in achieving your dreams?

 Once you replace negative thoughts with positive ones, you'll start having positive results.

—Willie Nelson
(Grammy and Lifetime Achievement award-winning entertainer)

STRATEGIES FOR ONLINE COLLEGE SUCCESS: AN OVERVIEW

Beginning any college course can be a complicated experience. Online learning offers its own challenges and rewards. Your path may have led you to online learning after years away from school or technology. It is important to recognize that although all individuals have a desire for success, nearly all also encounter roadblocks along the way. This textbook is designed to give you practical information and tools to make your online learning experience innovative, enriching, and successful.

Chapter 1 provides a general overview of elements that are important to online learning success. It is designed to give you a big picture of what constitutes success in an online learning environment. The chapters that follow will fill in the details of the success strategies outlined here.

POSITIVISM

Successful online students believe they will succeed. They approach the online experience as a challenge that they will gladly meet. Phrases such as "I can't" or "they didn't" are not in their vocabulary. They look for the good intentions of their faculty. They interpret feedback as constructive and intended to be helpful. They are interested in getting to know their peer group. They approach collaborative learning projects with enthusiasm. When confronted with real or perceived problems, they identify the "silver lining" and do something meaningful with it.

> ◢ REFLECTION QUESTION
>
> • What is your attitude toward higher education?

Apply **It!**

Positivism

Goal: To find positive role models and mentors.

STEP 1: Select your most positive relative or close friend. List the attributes this person has that led you to select him or her for this exercise.

STEP 2: Select an instructor, administrator, or other staff member in your online program who demonstrates a positive approach to life and work. List the attributes this person has that led you to select him or her for this exercise.

continued

STEP 3: Ask both of these individuals to be your e-learning coaches and work with you informally or formally to create or enhance your positive mental attitude.

STEP 4: Develop an electronic communication plan with your e-learning coaches. Perhaps your coach will agree to send an e-mail message to you once a week with an encouraging message. Or your coach may contact you through instant messenger (IM) every few days to see if you need a mental boost.

REFLECTION QUESTIONS

- What does a positive attitude mean to you?
- Consider the people you surround yourself with. Do they exhibit the attributes you ascribe to positivism?

CONNECTING WITH PEOPLE, WELL AND OFTEN

Often when online students don't succeed, it is due to the human element. They haven't connected with people who will mentor them to succeed. When you are an online student, you are not physically learning with others, so it is critical to establish a support network. Successful online students know the basics of establishing and maintaining good relationships. This can be done through e-mailing or instant messaging your faculty and peer network and through participation in chats and discussion boards.

 Apply **It!**

Connecting with People

Goal: To increase the scope of your interpersonal network.

STEP 1: Select three new prospective friends from your online peer group. Make your selection based on positivism, common interests, and/or shared goals.

STEP 2: Agree to ways in which you will communicate. For example, add them to your IM buddy list. Decide when you will be available to talk to each other online. Send e-mails to regularly exchange ideas on topics of mutual interest.

NEXT STEP THINKING

Online learning provides opportunities to research and explore topics of interest and career importance. Problem-based learning poses challenges and asks the student to find solutions. Successful online students use the information superhighway to the fullest and exceed requirements. They design creative projects and craft unique solutions to problems posed. They use the richness of the Internet to stimulate creative thought.

A SENSE OF TIMING

Successful online students understand their own needs and those of others, so they function effectively in diverse learning environments. They have developed the capacity to understand what is expected of them. They understand how to use both time and circumstance in pursuit of goals.

HAVING REACHABLE GOALS

Successful online students have clearly defined reasons they are studying online. They know what they plan to achieve and develop well-defined learning outcomes. Successful online students relate their online study to their personal goals. They understand how their online course or degree program will advance their career interests. Successful online students may "ladder" their degree goals. After the first goal is reached, then a new attainable goal may be projected.

Image copyright iofoto, 2009. Used under license from shutterstock.com

THE IMPORTANCE OF EDUCATION

As technology advances, society and industry must adapt and learn. Changes in consumer demand, technology, and many other factors will contribute to the continually changing employment structure in the economy.

The U.S. Department of Labor's Bureau of Labor Statistics' report on Tomorrow's Jobs projects that 18.9 million jobs will be added by 2014. As of December 20, 2005, a dozen of the fastest growing occupations required either a bachelor's or a associate's degree:

- Network systems and data communications analysts
- Physician assistants
- Computer software engineers
- Physical therapist assistants
- Dental hygienists

> Systems software workers
> Network and computer systems administrators
> Database administrators
> Forensic science technicians
> Veterinary technologists and technicians
> Diagnostic medical sonographers
> Occupational therapist assistants

Source: http://www.bls.gov/oco/print/oco2003.htm, Education and Training

Check the Bureau of Labor Statistics Web site frequently for updates on employment projections, wages, and educational requirements: http://www.bls.gov.

THE VALUE OF A COLLEGE DEGREE IN TODAY'S WORKFORCE

As you just learned, the value of a degree in today's workforce means remaining vital in tomorrow's workforce. However, a college degree can have immediate and far-reaching implications to your current job. Employers look for enthusiastic self-starters who embrace changing technology. Enrolling in an online college shows your employer you are serious about furthering your education. As you will see in Chapter 8, the U.S. Department of Labor also reports a direct correlation between increased education and increased earnings potential.

> REFLECTION QUESTIONS

- How could an advanced certification or degree help you in your career?
- What do you think your boss would think about an employee who was pursuing higher education?

Image copyright Andresr, 2009. Used under license from shutterstock.com

DISTANCE EDUCATION AND ACCREDITATION

In the United States, distance degree programs are accredited by a regional accrediting agency (the Distance Education and Training Council) or profession-sponsored accrediting agencies. With so many agencies, the potential for fraud gave birth to diploma mills.

Diploma mills have sprung up to meet the increasing demands of students looking for online education with fast results, but they have cut out everything between the "tuition" and the "diploma." Essentially, a diploma mill "degree" is bought, not earned. They may claim extraordinarily fast tracks to completion and below industry-standard tuition. Applying for a job with a phony degree is punishable as fraud and could include a fine or imprisonment. Keep in mind that if a degree program sounds too good to be true, it probably is.

Some of these diploma mills may claim accreditation. To know if the claimed accreditation has merit, you must look to lists of agencies recognized by the U.S. Department of Education (governmental recognition) and/or the Council on Higher Education Accreditation (educational industry recognition). You can conduct a search for accredited universities at http://www.ope.ed.gov/accreditation or get help from a consultant at http://www.degreefinders.com.

CAREER BENEFITS OF ONLINE LEARNING

The opportunity to study online will positively impact the career of hundreds of thousands of American workers. Individuals who are willing and able to further their learning are most likely to be successful.

Years ago, nontraditional learners were confronted with the daunting choice of resigning from employment to enroll in college or foregoing the opportunity to gain an education and get ahead. Technological advances have created conditions in which work and degree are compatible. Today's online learners can complete a college education from home, work, or a library computer at any time of the day or night.

MORE SKILLS

Online learners develop skills and gain experiences that make them more valuable to their employers. These include job-specific skills, as well as vital technical, professional, and interpersonal skills. A

Image copyright Chris Ryan, 2009. Used under license from shutterstock.com

workforce composed of such well-developed employees is good for the individuals and also for the reputation of the company as a whole.

BETTER PAY

Online learners may receive pay increases from their employers because they have completed a certification or degree. If your boss doesn't know about your educational pursuits, you should bring them up during your next review. You may also want to look into the qualifications of personnel at higher wage levels—you may have achieved the skills you need to graduate into the next wage tier at your company.

JOB ADVANCEMENT

It is often important to increase your credentials to reach the next level. Online learners are positioned to be selected for advancement due to their ambition to complete coursework online. Online learners distinguish themselves from their peers by their interest in learning and their willingness to gain it while simultaneously meeting the needs of their employers.

JOB SECURITY

When times get tough, and the market requires the workforce to shrink, employees with a strong work ethic and the best skills are

Image copyright Aurelio, 2009. Used under license from shutterstock.com

Image copyright Mike Tolstoy / photobank.kiev.ua, 2009. Used under license from shutterstock.com

most frequently retained by their employers. In the event that you must leave your current position, after you complete your degree, doors will open to you from outside the company. If your current employer cannot meet industry-standard wages for your new skills and qualifications, another employer can.

TAKING RESPONSIBILITY FOR YOUR EDUCATION

Taking responsibility for your education begins with setting goals and getting organized. You follow that up by staying focused and motivated on the goals that you have set.

SETTING GOALS

Setting goals is crucial to your success in online learning. By setting goals, you plan a "roadmap" for what you want to achieve and how you want to get there. Breaking long-term goals into shorter-term goals allows you to see progress. For example, your long-term goal

REFLECTION QUESTIONS

- What are your long-term and short-term goals? What are you trying to accomplish?
- Why is school important to your goals?

might be to get your certificate or degree. By plotting out a schedule for completion of classes or specific assignments, each class or assignment becomes a short-term goal. This brings you the recognition and reward of moving toward your long-term goal.

Goal setting is a series of sequential steps. You identify your goals, make an action plan to achieve them, and set new goals based on what you learn along the way.

success steps

The following success steps are based on suggestions made by Donohue (n.d.) for effective goal setting and achievement:

STEP 1: Set goals based on something that is important to you and something that you desire. Avoid letting someone else determine what your goals should be.

STEP 2: Make sure that your goals are complementary and do not conflict with one another.

STEP 3: In addition to professional areas, set goals that support spiritual, emotional, physical, and social needs.

STEP 4: State goals positively. For example, "I will study every night for two hours before checking my personal e-mail" is more positive than "I won't do other tasks in the evening before studying."

STEP 5: Be as detailed and specific as possible when writing your goals. Goals should tell you what you will achieve, describe the conditions under which you will achieve the goal, and provide a time frame during which the goal will be achieved. In addition, goals should be measurable so that you meet a standard. For example, "I will study [what will be achieved] for two hours [measurable element] every weekday night [another measurable element] with no interruptions [conditions] throughout the fall semester [time frame]."

STEP 6: Set your goals high enough to be challenging, but make them reasonable enough to be achievable.

STEP 7: State your goals in writing. Written goals serve as a reminder and motivator and provide a guide to your success. Telling others about your goals may also contribute to goal achievement.

1

Image copyright Liv friis-larsen, 2009. Used under license from shutterstock.com

GETTING MOTIVATED AND STAYING THAT WAY

Your attitude toward success directly impacts your academic and life experiences. As in many other areas of life, school will have its ups and downs, and there are times when you will encounter difficulties. Do not let problems become a roadblock to your success. Individuals who are able to use difficulties as learning opportunities will be valued in the classroom and by employers.

Learning to remain motivated during difficult situations is a valuable lesson that will make a difference to your success in school and every other aspect of your life.

▶ REFLECTION QUESTIONS

- What motivates you to learn?
- How can you use your motivators to help you reach your education goals?

success steps

Consider the following steps for maintaining your motivation:

1. Clearly identify your motivators.

2. Ensure that your motivators are realistic. For example, if you identify a reward for yourself, make sure it is something you can realistically do or afford.

3. Keep your motivators "top of the mind" so that they remain visible and you are aware of them.

1

GETTING THE MOST OUT
OF EVERY CLASS

REFLECTION QUESTIONS

- What do you want and hope to get out of each of your classes?
- What specific things can you do to make sure you get the most out of every class?

Getting the most from every class has specific benefits, including acquiring the most education for your investment of time and money, preparing to the best of your ability for your future career, and achieving self-improvement. Fully participating in and being actively involved in your classes allows you to gain a better perspective on and appreciation of others' beliefs and ideals. The diversity in today's workforce requires that you develop an understanding and acceptance of a wide range of cultures, beliefs, lifestyles, and other unique aspects of individuals.

GETTING ORGANIZED

Becoming organized can be quite challenging for some students. The concept of being organized can vary considerably between individuals. Organization includes the components of time and materials management as well as the ability to manage tasks and information efficiently. Chapter 1 and the remaining chapters in *100% Online Student Success* address these elements in greater detail. For now, consider how these components contribute to your organizational skills and which elements might be important for you to improve.

The first step toward improving organizational abilities is understanding your need to improve and determining where improvement is needed. Organization can impact function at home, in school, and at work. In addition, organization is a key factor in learning. The brain processes well-organized information more efficiently than information that is presented in random order. Your ability to organize information will directly affect your mastery of course information. To get the most out of each of your classes, try implementing the following organizational steps:

success steps

DEVELOPING ORGANIZATIONAL SKILLS

STEP 1: Assess your current organizational skills and then develop an action plan to improve where needed.

1

STEP 2: Use the Internet as a resource to develop your organizational skills. Conduct a search using "organizational skills" and "organizational methods," and select resources that are relevant to your needs.

STEP 3: Begin to work on organizing your classroom activities, study areas, times for studying and completing homework, and so forth. Select filing and archiving systems that work for you.

STEP 4: Develop charts, diagrams, flow charts, tables, lists, and other tools that can help organize the information you are trying to learn.

STEP 5: Don't procrastinate. Take the necessary time to complete assignments and projects thoroughly and well. Procrastination results in the need to rush, and rushing can create disorganized work.

STEP 6: Complete assignments on or ahead of an established schedule so that you have time to think them through in a well-organized fashion as well as review them.

TIME MANAGEMENT FOR ONLINE LEARNING

Many online students have very full lives, including work, family, home, personal responsibilities, and community responsibilities. Finding the time to accomplish all of this can be overwhelming.

Good time management starts with assessing what must typically be accomplished for each day and the time available to complete each task. For detailed time management strategies, see Chapter 7.

> ▶ REFLECTION QUESTIONS
>
> - How effective are your organizational skills?
> - What organizational strategies work well for you? How can they be applied to organizing for school?

Apply **It!**

Web Research

Goal: To research time management tools offered online.

STEP 1: Conduct an Internet search using "electronic time management tools" as your search term. Explore types of tools that are available.

continued

1

REFLECTION QUESTIONS

- Are there times in the day when you feel more productive than others?
- Are you aware of any potential "time-zapping" habits you could tone down? These could include surfing the Internet, checking personal e-mail, and watching television.

STEP 2: Explore the time management tools that you find as a result of your search. Assess and compare the benefits and shortcomings of each based on your personal needs and preferences. Make a decision regarding which would be support your time management efforts.

STEP 3: See if any of the tools are available as a free download or as a trial shareware. Give it a try, and see if it works well for you.

There are a variety of tools available for time and life management that are compatible with your online education. Electronic planning systems, including calendars, memos, and reminders, are available with your computer's operating system or word-processing software. If you carry a personal digital assistant (PDA) or cell phone, these mobile devices also have time management features. As a bonus, you can usually synchronize the features on the portable devices with those on your laptop or desktop computer to keep everything organized.

CHAPTER SUMMARY

This chapter introduced you to the strategies it takes to succeed as an online learner. It emphasized foundation elements, including positivism, communication, and next-step thinking, as well as practical requirements such as time management, goal setting, and personal organization. These basic self-management tools will lay the groundwork for developing and refining your skills using the information and activities in the remainder of *100% Online Student Success*.

POINTS TO KEEP IN MIND

In this chapter, several main points were discussed in detail:

- ❯ Successful online students believe they will succeed. They are infused with positivism.
- ❯ Communication is a vital skill, and for online students in particular, it's critical to develop a peer support network.

1

- ❯ Advances in technology continue to have an impact on the need for new jobs and individual skill requirements.
- ❯ Some career benefits of online education include more skills, better pay, job advancement, and job security.
- ❯ It's important to look into the accreditation of the online school you choose.
- ❯ Taking responsibility for your education begins with an assessment of your goals, attitudes, and motivation.
- ❯ Setting goals should include both short-term steps and long-term plans.
- ❯ Written goals that are specific and measurable are more likely to be accomplished than unwritten and unspecific goals.
- ❯ Individuals who see opportunity in and learn from difficulties will be valued in and out of the classroom.
- ❯ Time management requires focusing on what needs to be accomplished and determining the amount of time available for each task.

LEARNING OBJECTIVES REVISITED

Review the learning objectives for this chapter, and rate your level of achievement for each objective using the rating scale provided. For each objective on which you do not rate yourself as a 3, outline a plan of action that you will take to fully achieve the objective. Include a time frame for this plan.

1 = did not successfully achieve objective

2 = understand what is needed, but need more study or practice

3 = achieved learning objective thoroughly

	1	2	3
Explain what is meant by *positivism*.	☐	☐	☐
Explain the importance of education amid a changing economy.	☐	☐	☐
Describe how to identify whether an online college is accredited and how to avoid a "diploma mill."	☐	☐	☐
Describe four ways that higher education can positively impact your career.	☐	☐	☐

Explain the importance and process of goal setting.   ☐ ☐ ☐

Describe the impact that attitude and motivation can have on your academic success.   ☐ ☐ ☐

Explain and demonstrate an understanding of time management.   ☐ ☐ ☐

Steps to Achieve Unmet Objectives

Steps   Due Date

1. _____   _____

2. _____   _____

3. _____   _____

4. _____   _____

5. _____   _____

6. _____   _____

7. _____   _____

REFERENCES

Bureau of Labor Statistics. (n.d.) *Education and Training*. Retrieved from, http://www.bls.gov/oco/print/oco2003.htm

Chopra, D. (1991). *The Seven Spiritual Laws of Success*. Amber-Allen Publishing, Inc.

Coleman, S. (n.d.) *Why do students like online learning?* WorldWide-Learn. Retrieved from, http://www.worldwidelearn.com/education-articles/benefits-of-online-learning.htm

Donohue, G. (n.d.) *Goal Setting: Powerful Written Goals in 7 Steps!* Top Achievement. Retrieved from, http://www.topachievement.com/goalsetting.html]

Dyer, W. (2004). *The Power of Intention*. Hay House Inc.

Guilbert, S. D. (2001). *How to be a successful online student*. McGraw-Hill.

Hill, N. (1928). *The law of success in sixteen lessons*. Ralston University Press.

Hill, N. (2004.) *Think and Grow Rich!: The Original Version, Restored and Revised*. Aventine Press.

Light, R. J. (2001). *Making the most of college*. Harvard University Press.

McGuire, J. (n.d.) Importance of college education. CollegeView. Retrieved from, http://www.collegeview.com/importance_of_college-education.html

Sheeley, N. (2006). *Soul Medicine*. Elite Books.

Wahlstrom, Williams & Shea. (2003). *The successful distance learning student*. Wadsworth/Thomson Learning.

Wattles, W. (2006). *The Science of Getting Rich*. Filiquarian Publishing, LLC.

White & Baker. (2004). *The student guide to successful online learning*. Pearson Education, Inc.

CHAPTER OUTLINE

Overview of Online Communication and Community

Unique Aspects of Online Communication

Introducing Web 2.0

Establishing Identity

Online Etiquette

First and Last(ing) Impressions

2

Online Communication and Community

LEARNING OBJECTIVES

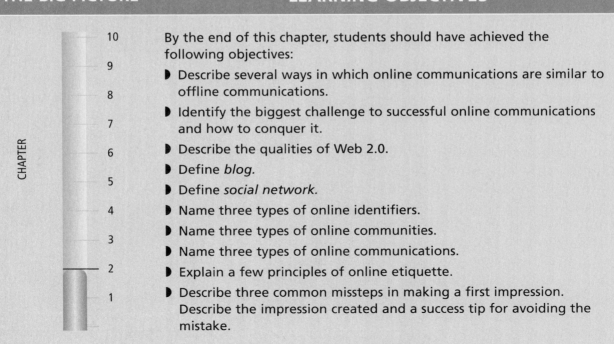

CHAPTER

10
9
8
7
6
5
4
3
2
1

By the end of this chapter, students should have achieved the following objectives:

▶ Describe several ways in which online communications are similar to offline communications.

▶ Identify the biggest challenge to successful online communications and how to conquer it.

▶ Describe the qualities of Web 2.0.

▶ Define *blog*.

▶ Define *social network*.

▶ Name three types of online identifiers.

▶ Name three types of online communities.

▶ Name three types of online communications.

▶ Explain a few principles of online etiquette.

▶ Describe three common missteps in making a first impression. Describe the impression created and a success tip for avoiding the mistake.

2

TOPIC SCENARIO

Greta works at a public relations firm and is trying to start her own business. She has enrolled in an online college to develop her business skills. Greta is naturally outgoing and a people person. These attributes have brought her career success but have left her feeling isolated academically.

Greta knows that there are other people in her degree program, but she doesn't know much about them. Interaction is mainly one-on-one between each student and the instructor. Although this individualized approach works well for some people, Greta is feeling cut off from her peers. She has decided to set up a bulletin board for the class and plans to e-mail the other students. She hopes they will join the bulletin board.

Based on Greta's situation, answer the following questions:

▶ In what ways could Greta's outgoing qualities benefit her in online education?

▶ What are the other ways that Greta could reach out to the other students in her program?

▶ Think about your own situation. How have you interacted socially and formed communities in and out of academics?

Image copyright Marcin Balcerzak, 2009. Used under license from shutterstock.com

2

 What should young people do with their lives today? Many things, obviously. But the most daring thing is to create stable communities in which the terrible disease of loneliness can be cured.

—*Kurt Vonnegut, Jr.*
(American writer)

OVERVIEW OF ONLINE COMMUNICATION AND COMMUNITY

Online learning creates opportunities and poses challenges when it comes to establishing community. The social fabric of communicating changes…or does it? Face-to-face communication is replaced by instant messages. Conversations turn into blogs with comments and trackbacks. Body language swaps out for emoticons. There is an electronic equivalent for almost all forms of physical interaction. For example, there's a "hug shirt" that transmits a touch sensation to the wearer wirelessly by cell phone. Although it's still in concept at http://www.cutecircuit.com, *Time Magazine* called it one of the best inventions of 2006.

REFLECTION QUESTIONS

- How do you define "community"?
- How do you feel about technology?
- How can technology help to create communities?

OPPORTUNITIES

Forward thinking, innovation, and creative problem solving are all huge components of online communication and community building. Although there may be an initial adjustment period to electronic communications, many people (students and nonstudents alike) are discovering that they may just prefer it. People feel immediately disconnected without their cell phones, smart phones, or laptops. The instant gratification of e-mail helped give the USPS system the nickname "snail mail." Previously isolated individuals can join online groups without ever leaving their homes. And judging by the popularity of social networking sites such as http://www.myspace.com and http://www.facebook.com, that is exactly what they're doing.

CHALLENGES

Have you ever been talking to someone in person or on the phone who said to you, "I can't read your expression" or "I can't read your tone"? Although you were part of a dialogue, you were having trouble getting the nuances of your feelings or point across. An amplified version of this problem is the single biggest challenge to successful online communication. That's because online communication is devoid of facial expressions, intonations, and body language. Your conversation partner cannot see you sweating, blushing, smiling, or fidgeting. The potential for misunderstanding looms large.

INTRODUCING WEB 2.0

REFLECTION QUESTIONS

- Are there opportunities you feel have passed you by due to lack of finances?
- In what ways could you integrate real-world hobbies and interests into the virtual world of the Internet?

That said, limitless opportunities for personal expression trump the potential for misunderstanding with Web 2.0. So coined by O'Reilly Media in 2004 to designate a second-generation of Web-based collaborative communities, Web 2.0 is a fertile environment for online learners. It's a refreshingly social approach to generating and distributing content. Open communication, decentralized authority, and freedom to create, publish, share, and reuse content characterize Web 2.0. Web 2.0 puts users in charge of their Internet experience (O'Reilly, 2005).

BLOGGING AND ONLINE JOURNALING

Blogs (short for web logs) and *online journals* are Web pages where an individual posts whatever is on his or her mind, from the personal to the political. A typical blog combines text, images, and links to other blogs, Web pages, and video. Readers post comments, and a virtual dialogue takes shape. Some blogs have themes like gadgets or travel.

Image copyright 7016366030, 2009. Used under license from shutterstock.com

Other blogs have penetrated the mainstream media and have loyal followings for breaking coverage of national news.

Start your own blog or online journal at any of the following Web sites:

▶ http://blog.com

▶ http://wordpress.com

▶ http://www.livejournal.com

Read blogs at these Web sites:

▶ http://www.technorati.com

▶ http://www.icerocket.com

SOCIAL NETWORKING

Social networks are online community groups offering an interactive network of friends, personal profiles, blogs, photos, music, and videos. Users generally start by "friending" people they know and then by extension, get acquainted with friends of friends. You can also search for friends based on similar interests. Social networking has become such a popular form of getting to know people that most bands, celebrities, and new movies have their own pages at http://www.myspace.com. A 2006 *Fortune* article showed MySpace as having the biggest market share of the social networks with 82% of the traffic and 230,000 new members daily (Sellers, 2006).

Join a social network at any of the following Web sites:

▶ http://www.myspace.com

▶ http://www.facebook.com

▶ http://www.tribe.net

Apply It!

Social Network Research

Goal: To explore social networks.

STEP 1: Choose one of the social networks in the preceding list, or pick one of your own by conducting an Internet search on "social networks."

continued

STEP 2: Use the social network's search engine to search for your classmates, friends, family, bands, or anyone or anything that piques your interest.

STEP 3: Think about how you feel about the network you chose. Try repeating these steps with another social network.

SOCIAL BOOKMARKING

Social bookmarking is a way for Web 2.0 users to store, classify, share, and search Internet bookmarks. These lists can be accessible to the public by users of a specific network or Web site. Other users with similar interests can view the links by topic or tags. Social bookmarking is particularly useful to share links to research with other students working on a group project.

Start bookmarking on these sites:

▶ http://reddit.com

▶ http://del.icio.us

▶ http://digg.com

SHARING PHOTOS

Photos can put faces to your virtual classmates. On a larger scale, photos give you a glimpse into diverse cultures you may not have

▶ REFLECTION QUESTION

• How could social networking and social bookmarking be useful in communicating with your online classmates?

Image copyright Cecilia Lim H M, 2009. Used under license from shutterstock.com

2

experienced. Photo-sharing networks differ as vastly as blogs—from personal candids to feats of photojournalism.

Start sharing photos at these sites:

▶ http://www.flickr.com

▶ http://www.snapfish.com

▶ http://www.photobucket.com

SELF-PUBLISHING

Prior to the advent of Web 2.0, if you wanted to design clothing or publish books, you had to shell out a bunch of money upfront to cover the costs of the setup and creation for more items than you probably needed. Even if you could find a place to do a small batch, the costs were still prohibitive. All that has changed. You can now be a published author or designer with just one t-shirt or book. Consider the uses for such publishing tools for your online education. You can have custom mouse pads printed for the class or turn your latest research project into a slick, coffee table book.

Start designing at these sites:

▶ http://www.cafepress.com

▶ http://www.blurb.com

▶ http://www.zazzle.com

Image copyright Andresr, 2009. Used under license from shutterstock.com

Apply **It!**

Design Time

Goal: To see how easy it is to design your own products online.

STEP 1: Go to http://www.cafepress.com, and click Make Your Own Stuff.

STEP 2: Choose something to make: clothes, mugs, cards, and so on, and click the icon. (You will not have to purchase the item.)

STEP 3: Browse your computer for a graphic, and upload it to the item.

STEP 4: Preview the design. Now think about how you could use this technology for school projects or class morale. Revisit the site with creative ideas.

Image copyright Johanna Goodyear, 2009. Used under license from shutterstock.com

WEBCASTING

Much like with publishing, Web 2.0 has brought broadcasting ability to the masses. You can record and publish your own video and audio broadcasts. YouTube is a popular video-sharing Web site where users can upload, view, and share video clips. *Webcasting*, sometimes called "podcasting," refers to digital media files designed for playback on portable media players. You can create content to webcast with just a digital camera and/or a microphone. Imagine the possibilities for class presentations.

Start webcasting at these sites:

▶ http://www.youtube.com

▶ http://www.apple.com/podcasting

▶ http://www.live365.com

ESTABLISHING IDENTITY

Perhaps you've been in a college class, company meeting, or retreat where you are paired up with a partner and asked to interview her and then present that person's story to the group. There are many versions of this, including groan-inducing "getting to know you" games with blindfolds and Post-it notes. Save for the extreme extroverts (see Chapter 4), most people not only dislike these forms of introduction but also end up feeling misrepresented.

With online communication, you can establish your identity on your own terms. Bygone are the days of feeling isolated and alone. Instant connections can be made via instant messenger (IM).

REFLECTION QUESTIONS

- How do you feel about the following statement: "People can be anyone they want on the Internet."
- Are there ways you can ensure you are talking to a "real" person?

TYPES OF ONLINE IDENTIFIERS

As described earlier, online learning and Web 2.0 offer an abundance of ways to stand out and be seen and heard. With all that self-expression, you need a place to park your creativity.

▶ **Personal Web pages**. Comprehensive information about you, including photos, blogs, and links to external content found on a social networking site, a Web site of your design, or a spot on the server your school maintains.

▶ **Profiles**. Typically, just your basic information found on a social network or e-mail group.

▶ **Signatures**. Signature files on forums should have a maximum height of 100 pixels, as to not cause clutter.

▶ **Avatars**. Pictures representing you, designed to make your digital interactions more expressive.

 Apply **It!**

Creating an Avatar

Goal: To create a 3D animated version of yourself for use online.

STEP 1: Go to http://www.meez.com.

STEP 2: Follow the directions to create, customize, and animate your Meez avatar.

STEP 3: Export your new avatar to your blog or Web page. Be sure to show your classmates.

TYPES OF ONLINE COMMUNITIES

There is an online community for every interest group from music to politics to cooking. You can join online communities based around your field of study. If you are enrolled in a nursing program, for instance, you will get valuable tips from community members

2

working in the medical industry. As you complete your degree, the contacts you made in the community could very well lead to jobs.

▶ **Social networks**. Online community groups offering an interactive network of friends, personal profiles, blogs, photos, music, and videos.

▶ **Discussion boards**. Bulletin boards with posts appearing in reverse order organized by topics (also known as threads).

▶ **Chat rooms**. A virtual room with a central theme that users come in to discuss.

TYPES OF ONLINE COMMUNICATION

Online communication helps you develop your written and interpersonal skills. There is no shortage of ways to interact online. Choose what works best for you.

▶ **E-mail**. Letters sent to individuals or group listservs.

▶ **Forums**. Posts and comments on blogs and bulletin boards.

▶ **Instant messenger (IM)**. Real-time communication between two or more people based on text typed over the Internet.

▶ **Chat rooms**. Similar to IM but takes place in a virtual "room" with several people at once.

▶ **Skype**. Voice and video conferencing over the Internet.

● ONLINE ETIQUETTE

Online etiquette (sometimes called "netiquette") refers to a code of conduct for use in e-mail and forum postings. Mind your manners in the following ways suggested on Wikipedia and http://www.dont-be-a-twit.com:

E-MAIL ETIQUETTE

▶ Use an informative subject heading.

▶ Use the to, cc, and bcc fields for what they were intended.

  ▶ To = The primary party for whom your message is intended, the person from whom you are expecting action and/or a reply.

2

▶ Cc = Other parties of interest to the correspondence but who do not necessarily have an active role.

▶ Bcc = People whose e-mail addresses you want to keep private and secure. Some or all of your correspondents may not want their addresses shared or risk exposure to spam and viruses.

▶ Most "flourishes" such as font colors and e-mail stationery simply scream amateur.

▶ Use emoticons and textspeak sparingly.

▶ Avoid sending inappropriate humor and chain letters.

FORUM ETIQUETTE

▶ Before creating a new topic, search to see if a similar topic already exists.

▶ Think before you post. It will soon be public, and you may not be able to delete it. Avoid angry and unnecessary posts that turn into "flame wars."

▶ Avoid crossposting the same information across multiple forums.

▶ Avoid using all capital letters. THIS IS CONSIDERED SHOUTING.

2

- How is online etiquette similar to face-to-face etiquette? How is it different?

▶ Don't embed pictures or files without permission.

▶ Use emoticons and textspeak sparingly.

▶ Quote brief excerpts from previous posts, enough to orient the reader only.

FIRST AND LAST(ING) IMPRESSIONS

You will want to give more careful thought to how you relate to others online. It can be easier to forget about relationship dynamics because you cannot see how others receive you. A perceived online "invisibility" can create conditions that contribute to reduced self-awareness.

The following are common missteps and ways to avoid them:

Mistake	Impression Created	Success Tip
Asking questions which demonstrate that you haven't read your syllabus and other posted introductory material.	You are careless or not sufficiently interested in the course to read what has already been provided.	Read syllabus carefully in advance of questioning your instructor regarding expectations. Only pose questions that suggest interest in the class.
Responding to getting acquainted exercises in a hurry.	You are an unimpressive student without goals, plans, or personality.	Introduce yourself to your instructor and your classmates in a way that communicates your strengths and your academic and personal goals. See the "Web 2.0" section of this chapter for some creative ways to get acquainted.
Doing a poor job on your first assignment.	Because this is the first sampling of your work, it is likely an indication of what you are capable of—for better or for worse.	Be certain to submit your early assignments completely, thoroughly, and on time. This will set the stage for you to be viewed as a serious, capable, student.
Using a tone in communications that suggests sarcasm, anger, or other negative emotions.	You are impolite at worst or careless and unconcerned at best.	Be certain to be polite and positive in all electronic communications. Use language to suggest that you are a confident, interested, capable, and collaborative learner.

SUMMARY

Online learning creates opportunities and poses challenges when it comes to establishing community. The biggest challenge is also the biggest opportunity—using the Internet for self-expression. Web 2.0 integrates with your online education seamlessly, allowing for an enriching array of open communication and freedom to create and share content. We hope this chapter has given you ideas on how you can reach out to your virtual classmates and start developing relationships and techniques that will help you both in school and in life.

POINTS TO KEEP IN MIND

In this chapter, several main points were discussed in detail:

- Forward thinking, innovation, and creative problem solving are all huge components of online communication and community building.
- Open communication, decentralized authority, and freedom to create, publish, share, and reuse content characterize Web 2.0, making it a fertile environment for online learners.
- Forms of self-expression on the Internet include blogging, online journaling, social networking, social bookmarking, sharing photos, self-publishing, and webcasting.
- Types of online identifiers include personal Web pages, profiles, signatures, and avatars.
- Types of online communities include social networks, discussion boards, and chat rooms.
- Types of online communication include e-mail, forums, IM, chat rooms, and Skype.
- Etiquette is as important online as it is offline.

LEARNING OBJECTIVES REVISITED

Review the learning objectives for this chapter, and rate your level of achievement for each objective using the rating scale provided. For each objective on which you do not rate yourself as a 3, outline a plan of action that you will take to fully achieve the objective. Include a time frame for this plan.

1 = did not successfully achieve objective

2 = understand what is needed, but need more study or practice

3 = achieved learning objective thoroughly

	1	2	3
Describe several ways in which online communications are similar to offline communications.	☐	☐	☐
Identify the biggest challenge to successful online communications and how to conquer it.	☐	☐	☐
Describe the qualities of Web 2.0.	☐	☐	☐
Define *blog*.	☐	☐	☐
Define *social network*.	☐	☐	☐
Name three types of online identifiers.	☐	☐	☐
Name three types of online communities.	☐	☐	☐
Name three types of online communications.	☐	☐	☐
Explain a few principles of online etiquette.	☐	☐	☐
Describe three common missteps in making a first impression. Describe the impression created and a success tip for avoiding the mistake.	☐	☐	☐

Steps to Achieve Unmet Objectives

Steps	Due Date
1. _____	_____
2. _____	_____
3. _____	_____
4. _____	_____
5. _____	_____
6. _____	_____
7. _____	_____

REFERENCES

O'Reilly, T. What is Web 2.0.: Design patterns and business models for the next generation of software. Retrieved September 30, 2005, from http://www.oreillynet.com/pub/a/oreilly/tim/news/2005/09/30/what-is-web-20.html

Sellers, P. Myspace cowboys. *Fortune*. Retrieved August 29, 2006, from http://money.cnn.com/magazines/fortune/fortune_archive/2006/09/04/8384727/index.htm

2

CHAPTER OUTLINE

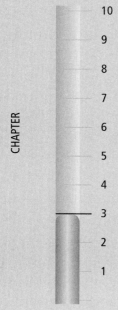

3

Technical Considerations

THE BIG PICTURE

LEARNING OBJECTIVES

By the end of this chapter, students should have achieved the following objectives:

- Describe the differences between a laptop and desktop computer.
- Explain what hardware and software are technical essentials for online learning.
- Define *operating system.*
- Describe the differences between the Microsoft Windows and Apple Macintosh operating systems.
- Describe the types of Internet connections and their advantages and disadvantages.
- Define *Web browser,* and name three.
- Describe how to save files and some of the differences between file formats.
- Explain how to download and upload files.
- Explain what questions you should ask when setting up an ergonomic home classroom.

TOPIC SCENARIO

Davida is shopping for a new computer for her online education program. She enjoys keeping up with technology but sometimes finds the constant changes and endless acronyms a little overwhelming. She is considering buying a laptop so that she can continue her studies when she goes on frequent business trips. She knows that most hotels and airports are equipped with WiFi hotspots that will keep her connected.

Davida polled her colleagues to see who owns Windows computers and who owns Macs and found the results to be about even. She wonders what advantages there really are to one or the other or if it is all just marketing hype.

Based on Davida's situation, answer the following questions:

▶ Where could Davida look to find out more information about the differences between the Windows and Mac operating systems?

▶ Thinking about Davida being a frequent traveler, do you agree with her thoughts on purchasing a laptop?

▶ Thinking about your lifestyle and responsibilities, do you think a desktop or laptop computer would best serve you?

❝ *"If you give people tools, [and they use] their natural ability and their curiosity, they will develop things in ways that will surprise you very much beyond what you might have expected."*

—Bill Gates,
CEO Microsoft

THE TECHNICAL ESSENTIALS

Online education is all about choice. Among many other flexible benefits, you have your choice of what courses to take, when to study, where to complete your assignments, and how to turn in your work. Your choices drive what technology you need. Getting your degree online can be a very frugal method of advancing your education. You may find that you require only a laptop, or you may want to assemble an entire virtual classroom. Whether you take a minimalist or materialistic approach to the technical essentials, you can still get what you need without breaking your budget.

CHOOSING EQUIPMENT TO MEET YOUR NEEDS

The desire for faster, smaller, smarter, sleeker, and safer technology makes the average useful life of a computer a fraction of that of your car. Yesteryear's bulky computer monitors look like paperweights in the current age of silver flat panels and slick LCD screens. Choosing technology as an investment in your education means embracing change, but learning to separate legitimate advancements from mere hype is important. According to an April 2007 article from *Computer World* entitled "Don't Believe the Hype: The 21 Biggest Technology Flops," even the major players (Apple, IBM, and Microsoft) make mistakes.

So how can you stay an informed consumer without falling prey to the latest marketing campaign? A simple approach is to research, comparison shop, and buy only what you really need.

REFLECTION QUESTIONS

- Do you consider yourself someone who keeps up with technology?
- How do you typically make informed choices about big purchases in your life (car, appliances, house, etc.)?

Image copyright 300dpi, 2009. Used under license from shutterstock.com

3

HARDWARE

The most crucial corporeal component of your online education is your computer. At one time, there were two types of computers: analog and digital. Today's computers are all digital, and they use a behind-the-scenes system of processing the numbers 1 (on) and 0 (off) to perform logical operations with amazing speed.

PERSONAL COMPUTERS

Personal computers are intended for general use by a single person. Although roommates, families, and colleagues can and do share personal computers, the "personal" designation separates the PC from a *server*—a more powerful computer that provides services to other computers over a network. It is important to note that the term "PC" has also become synonymous with a personal computer running the Microsoft operating system. There are three main kinds of personal computers:

▶ Desktop

▶ Laptop

▶ PDA

A desktop computer is typically the cornerstone of your virtual classroom or home office. Laptops are portable computers that take up less space and are great for travel. A personal digital assistant (PDA) may be convenient to have but is not an essential element of your virtual classroom.

Whether you own a computer or use one at work or the library, the computer will be the interface for your online program and keep you connected to your classmates. Like the price of gas, computer prices rise and fall. But thanks to a healthy amount of competition between manufacturers, connecting to your online college can be far more cost-effective than commuting to a traditional college campus.

Nearly all computer manufacturers (including Apple, Dell, HP, and Gateway) offer student discounts. Many companies also accept payment plans that render the need to lease a computer obsolete. Before purchasing a computer, research the brand and the features you need. For example, if you're going to be creating or using graphics

Image copyright Rui Vale de Sousa, 2009. Used under license from shutterstock.com

and video, you will need ample memory. If you will be running several programs at once, you will want a fast processor. You should also consider and compare customer service, technical support, bundled software, and warranty.

Personal Computers: A Personal Decision

Only a few years ago, the decision was black and white: Desktop computers were full-featured, and laptops were prohibitively expensive. However, with laptop prices declining and features increasing, how do you know whether a desktop or laptop PC is right for you?

> ▶ REFLECTION QUESTION
>
> • Think about how you will use your computer. Will you travel much with it? Will you need to connect many devices?

	Desktop	Laptop
Capability	• Fully functional hardware, drives, and ports for peripherals.	• Fully functional hardware, drives, and ports for peripherals.
Cost	• Less than a laptop with similar features.	• More than a desktop with similar features.
	• Service and repair costs are lower due to replaceable parts.	• Service and repair costs are higher due to all-in-one design.
Power	• Remains plugged in for constant power.	• Mid-range laptops have battery life of about four hours. AC power and additional and longer-range batteries are also available.

continued

3

	Desktop	Laptop
Portability	• Computer is not portable. • Files are easily portable with flash memory devices or by using services such as http://www.gotomypc.com.	• Lightweight; size of a notebook. • Great for travel; small spaces. • Convenient access to wireless Internet networks.
Durability	• Solid durability if maintenance is observed.	• Vulnerable to drops, spills, and theft.
Ergonomics	• Separate monitor and keyboard make for easier ergonomic customization.	• Add-on keyboards, mice, and docking stations can convert your laptop into a desktop.
Obsolescence	• Parts can be removed, replaced, and upgraded. • Peripherals can extend lifespan.	• Size and design limits upgrading options. • Peripherals are not always portable.

When researching a new computer purchase, check that it has at least the following standard features:

▶ 1GB RAM (Random Access Memory)

▶ 80GB – 100GB hard drive

▶ 4 USB (Universal Serial Bus) ports

▶ DVD-RW burner (plays and copies CDs and DVDs)

▶ Dual-core processor

▶ Latest operating system

▶ If laptop: less than 6 pounds

▶ If laptop: at least three hours of battery life

Anything else, such as graphics card, speakers, monitor size, and so on, is your preference.

PERIPHERALS

Your computer is the only true technical *essential*. However, there is no shortage of peripherals, or devices that connect to your computer, that could make your life more convenient.

▶ **Portable media storage**. This includes USB thumb, jump, or Flash drives. These are key chain-sized devices that can hold a few gigabytes of your files. Because the USB port is standard, it allows you to transfer files from one computer to another. For instance, if you needed to print out a project at a copy shop, you could save all of your files on a USB drive and plug it in to the computer at the copy shop.

- **Inkjet or laser printer**. Laser printers provide the quickest and cleanest output but can be expensive. For general-purpose color and black-and-white printing, inkjet printers are more affordable. When comparing models, factor in the cost of replacement ink cartridges too.

- **All-in-one printer/fax/scanner/copier**. All-in-one devices are tempting to buy because they take up just about the same footprint (space) as a printer but include faxing, scanning, and copying capabilities in addition. The negative to all-in-ones is the same criticism as that of laptops: if one part fails, the whole unit may need to be replaced.

- **Modem/router**. A modem is used for connecting to the Internet. This can be either a standard modem that you use with your existing phone lines for dial-up access, a DSL modem that also uses your phone line but does not tie up your line, or a cable modem that uses the same cable as your cable television. A router is used to network multiple wired computers or set up a wireless network, which is useful for laptops.

- **Ergonomic mouse and keyboard**. Most likely, the keyboard and mouse that came with your desktop or laptop are not the best fit for your hands. A variety of keyboards and mice with ergonomic features are available. Go to a computer supply store and try out different models to see what feels the most comfortable.

- **Digital camera**. If your schoolwork has a creative element, you can justify this peripheral. A digital camera makes it easy for you to personalize projects and Web pages alike.

Image copyright Jeffrey Van Daele, 2009. Used under license from shutterstock.com

REFLECTION QUESTIONS

- How might having a digital camera or webcam make you feel more connected to your online classmates?
- Can you think of any other peripherals that you might want/need to add to your home classroom?

OPERATING SYSTEMS

An operating system (OS) is a set of computer programs that manages the hardware and software resources of a computer. The OS forms a platform for other system and application software. The "user" of an OS is an application, not a person. Most personal computers have a graphical user interface (GUI), like the "windows" in Windows XP. When you double-click an icon or use the File menu to open a program, that system of 0s and 1s mentioned earlier is working behind the scenes to fulfill your request.

Image copyright Andresr, 2009. Used under license from shutterstock.com

WINDOWS XP AND VISTA

Microsoft Windows was first introduced in 1985 as a GUI add-on to command-line MS-DOS in response to growing requests for a GUI. An estimated 525 million personal computer users are running Microsoft Windows XP, and most are expected to eventually upgrade to the latest Windows OS, Vista (Droz, 2005).

But it's been a somewhat rocky road for Microsoft. In the late 90s, viruses and security threats commonly plagued the Windows OS. Then, in November 1999, a federal judge declared that by possessing a 90% share of the personal computer market, Microsoft Corp. harmed consumers through its anticompetitive behavior (Moore, 1999).

However, the market share remains strong today, and there are reasons for that. Microsoft's operating system supports a variety of software and hardware. Microsoft Office is the standard for business productivity software and includes programs for creating documents, spreadsheets, graphics, and presentations. Peripherals that plug into the Microsoft environment are priced competitively and can often be less expensive than comparable Apple OS products.

MAC OS X

Mac OS X is the successor to the original Mac OS, which had been Apple's primary operating system since 1984. There has always been a great debate between Mac and Windows die-hards on which is the superior OS. Starting in 2006, the "Get a Mac" advertising campaign

3

hit TVs and has grown to more than two dozen ads in the United States, United Kingdom, Canada, and Japan. The ads feature personifications of a Mac and a Windows PC and highlight the PC's flaws with sharp satire. The ads were created for Apple, by TBWA, an ad agency operating around the world out of New York. You can view the ads at http://www.apple.com/getamac or by searching http://www.youtube.com.

Many people find that Apple computers are simpler to set up and maintain. Since the release of the iMac in 1998, Apple computers began a steady increase in popularity among students seeking affordable and aesthetic options. Fashionable colors and rounded edges replaced the beige blocky old PC monitors. The iMac's CPU was integrated into its egg-shaped monitor making a separate tower obsolete. The even smaller footprint of subsequent editions of the iMac was perfect for the cramped quarters of a dorm room.

Macs are not the cheapest option but with their outstanding security and on-board suite of software, they may keep costs down over the course of ownership. A computer running the Mac OS also gives users the flexibility to read and write almost all Windows files, including Microsoft Office documents. Many students who use Macs as their first computer find it easier to use a Windows PC later if a job calls for the switch.

REFLECTION QUESTIONS

- What do you know about the Mac OS? Who/what do you think it is good for? Who/what do you think it is bad for?
- What do you know about the Microsoft OS? Who/what do you think it is good for? Who/what do you think it is bad for?

Apply **It!**

Mac vs. PC

Goal: To learn more about the differences between the Mac and Windows operating systems and the people who use them.

STEP 1: Watch the "Get a Mac" commercials at http://www. apple.com/getamac or by searching http://www.youtube. com. How do you feel about the way the Mac and PC are represented? Which of the "characters" seem more like you?

STEP 2: As you interact with friends and colleagues, see if you can guess whether they have a Mac or PC. What characteristics are you basing your guesses on? Are your guesses founded in facts?

STEP 3: Ask people what kinds of personal computers they have. Try to ask open questions, such as "How is Microsoft Vista working out for you?" You may find you meet people who have neither Macs nor PCs, but Linux instead.

STEP 4: Record your observations in a chart on your computer. Are Macs better than PCs for certain activities? Are PC people different from Mac people?

SOFTWARE

Software is the umbrella term for programs that interact with your OS and increase your productivity. You can get software to help you do your taxes, create music, or play games. We will focus on the types of software essential to your online learning experience.

WORD-PROCESSING SOFTWARE

Word-processing software is the suite of programs that allows you to create documents, format spreadsheets, and make presentations. Often, the programs come with templates for writing business letters, sending faxes, and setting up basic Web pages. Your computer may come with a very basic word-processing program already installed.

Most students will need to upgrade to a suite such as Microsoft Office. The 2007 version of Microsoft Office integrates communications and Web services with standard applications. A few of the software features include the following:

▶ Word for document creation (and now blogging)

▶ Outlook for e-mail (and now text messages)

▶ Excel for organized spreadsheets

▶ PowerPoint for multimedia presentations

Microsoft Office is available for both Mac and Windows computers. You can download a free trial or use a browser-based version at http://www.Office2007.com.

Google has recently entered the word-processing domain with a free collection of online productivity tools called Google Apps. Google Apps have mobile and online students in mind. With Google Apps, you have access to e-mail, contacts, calendar, and instant messaging anywhere, anytime. The education suite can help your virtual campus community work together more effectively. There is no software to download. A few of the features include the following:

▶ E-mail at your school's domain (student@your-school.edu) with 2GB of storage per account

▶ Sharable calendars to coordinate class schedules, meetings, and campus events

▶ Google Docs & Spreadsheets to create and collaborate on documents from any computer, anywhere in the world

◗ Google Talk for free instant messaging, file sharing, and voice calling around the world

Learn more about whether Google Apps is right for you at http://www.google.com/a/.

Apply **It!**

Software Research

Goal: *To compare popular software productivity suites and see what meets your needs.*

STEP 1: Think about what you need out of a productivity suite for school: document creation, e-mail, spreadsheets, presentations, and so on.

STEP 2: Compare the features in Microsoft Office 2007 with those in Google Apps by reading their Web site information at http://www.Office2007.com and http://www.google.com/a, respectively.

STEP 3: Create a document outlining the available features and those that you need.

STEP 4: If neither product was right for you, start a new Internet search for "word processing software" and "office software." You may be able to find additional freeware and shareware at http://www.download.com.

COMPUTER AND INTERNET SECURITY

You lock the doors to your home and your car, so it makes sense that you also want to protect your computer. Many programs are available that enhance and defend the performance of your computer with tools to remove Internet clutter and temporary files, recover deleted files, and protect against spyware and viruses.

A critical consideration for always-on Internet (see "The Need for Speed" section later in this article) connections is the potential for hackers to cause trouble on your computer. For this reason, a *firewall* is recommended. Firewalls protect your network from unauthorized entry, allowing only the users you designate to access the network (and your computer) over the Internet. The firewall software recognizes perceived attacks and blocks unauthorized users.

Image copyright Feng Yu, 2009. Used under license from shutterstock.com

▶ Learn more about Norton Systemworks 2007 at http://www.symantec.com.

▶ Learn more about Internet Security Suite 2007 at http://www.mcafee.com/us.

Spyware

If you browse or download content from the Internet, your computer may have collected a few uninvited guests. *Spyware*—also called adware and malware—has become such a problem that an entire industry of "anti-spyware" software has sprung up to combat it.

When spyware finds its way onto your computer, it secretly records and transmits your personal information. It can log the keys that you type, record your Internet browsing habits, and scan documents on your hard drive. The effects of spyware range from criminal theft of passwords to being an unknowing participant in an advertising focus group.

Protect yourself by searching for anti-spyware at http://www.download.com or get started right away with the free Personal Edition of Ad-Aware SE at http://www.lavasoftusa.com.

OTHER SOFTWARE

Additional software depends on what you're studying. You may need to be able to create graphics or edit video, for instance. Your instructors will let you know what is required when you start the course. Don't forget to inquire about student discounts whether you order the software from the school or from its manufacturer. You can also find deep discounts on software at http://www.ebay.com, but you should take care to only purchase factory-sealed new products from reputable dealers with high feedback ratings.

INTERNET ACCESS

3

REFLECTION QUESTIONS

- How do you connect to the Internet currently?
- How could your connection be improved? Where could you find resources about changing or upgrading your Internet access?

The past few years have seen the cost of Internet access declining while entire cities and enterprising cafes clamor to provide wireless hotspots to match the demand. Major U.S. cities planning municipal WiFi (wireless fidelity) networks include San Francisco, Chicago, Denver, and Miami Beach (Grebb, 2005). It's not science fiction to think that within the next 10 years, the entire country could be blanketed in an invisible quilt of Internet access. But until then, let's discuss what you need to connect to your virtual classroom.

THE NEED FOR SPEED

There are four main ways for individuals to connect to the Internet, and they vary in speed and cost.

- **Dialup**. The highest speed that you can reach using analog is 56Kbps, which is fine for text and e-mail files but slow for accessing graphic-intensive Web sites or downloading large files. This is the least expensive option and is available anywhere there is a phone line. However, its biggest disadvantages are its slow speeds (particularly if the network is crowded) and its dedicated use of your phone line that will provide incoming callers with a constant busy signal.

- **DSL**. DSL provides very high-speed (over 100 times faster than dial-up) Internet access over standard telephone lines. DSL is always on and eliminates the wait-time of dial-up. DSL is priced at competitive monthly rates, and its availability in your area typically depends on your distance from the phone company.

- **Cable**. Cable modems achieve some of the highest data transfer speeds (up to 42Mbps downstream, 10Mbps upstream) by using the high-bandwidth capabilities of cable TV lines. Speeds can vary depending on traffic on the lines. Cable

Image copyright Eimantas Buzas, 2009. Used under license from shutterstock.com

3

providers often bundle cable Internet with cable TV packages. Shop around for a good deal.

▶ **Wireless broadband**. WiFi has taken high-speed Internet to the next level. With a wireless network card included in most laptops, you can achieve speeds of 256Kbps to as much as 10Mbps or more. The advantage is portability and free access at a local WiFi hotspot. You can also use a laptop wirelessly with either the DSL or cable network you already have in your home.

For more information about Internet access, types of connections, and determining what meets your needs best, visit http://www.broadbandinfo.com.

Apply **It!**

Test Your Speed

Goal: To analyze your computer's performance based on upload and download speed.

STEP 1: Go to http://www.dslreports.com.

STEP 2: Select Tools from the top navigation bar.

STEP 3: Select Speed Tests.

continued

STEP 4: Click Flash 8 plugin based speed test. You will be shown a list of servers running the speed test. Examine the choices for open slots and mileage from your location. Click your choice of server to begin the test.

STEP 5: Compare your actual download and upload speed results to those advertised by your ISP (Internet Service Provider). Follow the link to compare your results to other customers of your ISP in your area. If your computer is connecting at significantly slow speeds, you will need to call the ISP and run some tests (see the "Computer and Internet Security" section earlier in this chapter).

BROWSERS

A Web browser is a program that displays text, images, and other information on a Web page at a Web site on the Internet. Users can interact with the Web page by clicking *hyperlinks* and traveling to other pages and virtual destinations. Web browsers are an essential part of the online learners' toolkit. Through Web browsers, you can access search engines, research projects, read current news, and stay connected.

Some of the Web browsers available for personal computers include Internet Explorer, Firefox, Safari, Netscape, Opera, and Mozilla in descending order of popularity (Browser, 2007).

You're encouraged to download and experiment with different browsers. You will find that content often displays with subtle differences depending on browser and OS. Many browsers allow you to customize features, and some feature handy features such as tabs and widgets putting frequently viewed or needed information at your fingertips.

> ▶ REFLECTION QUESTION
>
> • What browser(s) do you currently use to view the Internet? Is there a standard that is used by the company you work for or the school you go to? Can you see any advantages to using multiple browsers?

YOUR HOME CLASSROOM

PC may stand for personal computer, but the "P" is in serious danger of having the word "personal" replaced with "portable." As you've just been reading, everything from Internet access to productivity software is being designed with mobility in mind. On a sunny day in the spring, why not set up shop on your balcony or patio with a wireless connection and your latest reading assignment? When traditional students are cramped into uncomfortable desks under fluorescent lights in a classroom, and you're reclining with your laptop on a chaise lounge, homework will feel like home but not work!

All kidding aside, it's a good idea to designate a part of your home as a classroom for a few reasons:

▶ You will want an ergonomic setup for when you have long hours of work ahead.

▶ You will want a quiet space to think, study, and participate in teleconferences.

▶ You need a rainy day alternative to the balcony or patio.

Your home classroom need not be big. If you already have a home office area, that is ideal. If not, you can use drapes or shoji screens to section off your classroom from the rest of the living space and potential distractions. You will need the following basics:

▶ A desk

▶ A chair

▶ A lamp

▶ A shelf for equipment, books, and supplies

Image copyright iofoto, 2009. Used under license from shutterstock.com

NOTEBOOK USERS TAKE NOTE

Note to laptop users: holding a laptop for hours isn't the most comfortable, safe, or ergonomic way to work. A lap desk can keep some heat off your lap and provide a stable surface for your laptop. Some lap desks include cooling systems that can plug into your laptop's USB port. Overheating is not ideal for you or the computer.

Try searching http://reviews.cnet.com for "laptop desk" and "laptop cooler" for recommendations.

BASIC COMPUTER SKILLS

We've come a long way from the time when personal computers took up entire rooms, and users communicated with them in complicated programming languages. These days, computers are compact and user-friendly. Although appearances and ways of interacting with computers are always changing, online students should be familiar with a few basic functions.

Saving Files

Most people regard saving their work as a no-brainer and can get belligerent at what they perceive as an obvious reminder…until there's a power outage, and they lose that 20-page paper they never took the seconds to save. Save early and often! Go to the File > Save menu from the application in which you're working, or use a keyboard shortcut such as Ctrl-S (PC) or Command-S (Mac).

You can save your files in many formats. How you save your file is determined by what type of file it is and what you plan to do with it. When you save your file, the title is appended with a short extension that tells the OS how to open it.

The most common way to save a word-processing document is with the Microsoft Word extension (.doc). However, there are instances when you might want to save your file in a different format. If you are e-mailing your resume, save it as plain text (.txt). If you want to preserve the formatting, save it in portable document format (.pdf).

Images also have file extensions. When you save images, such as those you took with a digital camera, bear in mind what you plan to do with them. Images that will be posted online or e-mailed are typically saved in compressed formats that reduce their file size. Photos are saved as .jpegs and illustrations as .gifs. Images that require high resolutions for printing or enlarging are saved uncompressed as .tif, .eps, or one of many proprietary image software formats.

For more information on how to save files and to learn about file extensions you encounter that are unfamiliar to you, check the frequently updated database, http://www.file-extensions.org.

Downloading Files

While on the topic of unfamiliar file extensions, we would be remiss to not issue a disclaimer. As with file saving, this is another reminder at which computer users tend to scoff. However, if everyone truly did this, the problem of computer viruses wouldn't be so pervasive. We've all heard the expression, "look before you leap." The technological take on that is "determine before you download." Do not download or open file formats you do not recognize, *especially* if you don't know the author/sender. One little click can initiate a chain reaction that damages your computer and the systems of people with whom you interact.

That said, file downloading is a great way to get information quickly. You can download books, music, movies, and more. Your instructor may post your syllabus or reading material online. To download a file, you click on it and tell your computer where to save it. Downloading is also an efficient way to transfer files among your peers. To share something of yours so that other students can download it, you will first need to upload it.

Uploading Files

Your instructor may establish an area on your course's Web site in which to save your completed assignments. To upload files, you will need a File Transfer Protocol (FTP) program. Many companies make FTP software. Some offer free FTP programs for academic use. Fetch is a popular FTP program among Mac users, and WS_FTP remains the standard among Windows users.

When you upload or download a file, two computers are involved: a server and a client. The FTP server, running FTP server software, listens on the network for connection requests from other computers. The client computer, running FTP client software, initiates a connection to the server. Once connected, you can upload your files to a directory and share them with other students.

You can also upload files to your personal Web site, as we discussed in Chapter 2. This is called *hosting*.

ERGONOMICS 101

Creating a good ergonomic working arrangement is an important part of protecting your health. As you set up your home classroom, ask yourself these questions provided by Cornell University's Ergonomics Web (Hedge, 2007):

▶ **Who will be using the computer?** If it's just you, optimize the desk, chair, and monitor height for you. If you are sharing the workstation, create an arrangement that satisfies all extremes, or consider separate chairs and an adaptable workstation.

▶ **Will you be using a desktop or a laptop computer?** Most desks are set up for desktop computers. If you will be using a laptop for a sustained period of time, an external keyboard and lap desk/docking station are recommended.

▶ **What type of desk are you using?** A good keyboard tray is the cornerstone of an ergonomic workstation. It allows you to type at a comfortable position that is neutral for your arms and wrists. Another option is the sit/stand desk. By adjusting a lever, the desk can be raised up to accommodate a standing position. A sit/stand desk encourages you to move and change positions regularly.

▶ **What type of chair are you using?** Choose a chair that has many ergonomic features: lumbar support, adjustable armrests, and levers for raising and tilting the seat to your preference.

▶ **What type of keyboard are you using?** Many ergonomic keyboards, mice, and wrist rests are available at computer stores. Before purchasing a product, see if there is research behind the claims that it is ergonomic. For most people, typing at the proper neutral position is the most important aspect of keyboard safety.

▶ **How is the light?** If the lighting is too bright or causes glare on the screen, you could develop eyestrain or headaches. Carefully consider your home classroom's lighting and add an anti-glare screen if needed.

▶ **How is your posture?** You should sit back in the chair with your feet touching the floor, your head and neck straight, and your wrists as flat as possible.

3

▶ **Does your workstation need any ergonomic add-ons?**
Many consumer products are marketed as ergonomic solutions. In general, you really need only what helps you achieve the recommended posture. This may include a footrest, a wrist rest, a stacker to raise your monitor to eye level, a lumbar support pillow for your back, and a document holder.

To review checklists prior to purchasing and setting up your workstation, visit the OSHA Web site at http://www.osha.gov. Select eTools from the Compliance Assistance menu, and then select Computer Workstations from the Ergonomics eTools list. From there, you can print a purchasing guide and ergonomic compliance checklist. Good health habits are the foundation for success and are discussed in depth in Chapter 7. If you are sick, uncomfortable, or in pain, even the fastest, slickest computer isn't going to help you in your quest for success.

CHAPTER SUMMARY

A personal computer is the gateway to your online learning experience. It is the platform on which you study assignments and complete projects, and it connects you to your classmates and an Internet full of information. Choosing between brands and types of computers is a personal decision based on preferences, features, cost, and comfort. Embracing technology means embracing change. Technology can be both exciting and overwhelming. Stick to your basic technology needs, and invest time and money in creating an ergonomic work environment that invites you to want to learn.

POINTS TO KEEP IN MIND

In this chapter, several main points were discussed in detail:

- ▶ Choosing technology as an investment in your education means embracing change, but learn to separate legitimate advancements from mere hype.

- ▶ Whether you own a computer or use one at work or the library, the computer will be the interface for your online program and keep you connected to your classmates.

3

▶ Purchasing a desktop or laptop computer and deciding on OS preference are personal choices.

▶ Basic word-processing and Internet security software are recommended essentials. Your instructor will inform you if additional software is necessary.

▶ Your Internet connection is dictated by your need for speed, finances, and availability of high-speed and wireless networks in your area.

▶ Creating a good ergonomic working arrangement is an important part of protecting your health.

LEARNING OBJECTIVES REVISITED

Review the learning objectives for this chapter, and rate your level of achievement for each objective using the rating scale provided. For each objective on which you do not rate yourself as a 3, outline a plan of action that you will take to fully achieve the objective. Include a time frame for this plan.

1 = did not successfully achieve objective

2 = understand what is needed, but need more study or practice

3 = achieved learning objective thoroughly

	1	2	3
Describe the differences between a laptop and desktop computer.	☐	☐	☐
Explain what hardware and software are technical essentials for online learning.	☐	☐	☐
Define *operating system*.	☐	☐	☐
Describe the differences between the Microsoft Windows and Apple Macintosh operating systems.	☐	☐	☐
Describe the types of Internet connections and their advantages and disadvantages.	☐	☐	☐
Define *Web browser*, and name three.	☐	☐	☐
Explain what questions you should ask when setting up an ergonomic home classroom.	☐	☐	☐
Describe how to save files and some of the differences between file formats.	☐	☐	☐
Explain how to download and upload files.	☐	☐	☐

Steps to Achieve Unmet Objectives

Steps   Due Date

1. _____   _____

2. _____   _____

3. _____   _____

4. _____   _____

5. _____   _____

6. _____   _____

7. _____   _____

● REFERENCES

Browser market share for year 2007. *Net Applications*. Retrieved
    May 13, 2007, from http://www.netapplications.com.

Droz, J. Mac vs. PC. Retrieved May 4, 2005, from http://www.
    killerbytes.com/Mac%20Advocacy/MACvsPCCombined.pdf.

Grebb, M. Cities unleash free WiFi. *Wired*. Retrieved October
    19, 2005, from http://www.wired.com/gadgets/wireless/
    news/2005/10/68999.

Hedge, A. Ergonomic guidelines for arranging a computer
    workstation - 10 steps for users. Cornell University Ergonomics
    Web. Retrieved March 16, 2007, from http://ergo.human.
    cornell.edu/ergoguide.html.

Moore, J. F. Federal judge says software firm possesses operating
    system monopoly. *CNN Money*. Retrieved November 5, 1999,
    from http://money.cnn.com/1999/11/05/technology/
    microsoft_finding.

CHAPTER OUTLINE

Success: A Personalized Path

Personality, Learning, and You

Personality Type

Personality Development

4 Your Uniqueness Factor

LEARNING OBJECTIVES

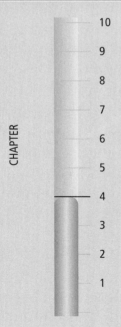

By the end of this chapter, students should have achieved the following objectives:

- Provide a definition for *personality*.
- Name the system for identifying different personality types based on the theories of Carl Jung.
- Explain the difference(s) between the Sensing and Intuition Preferences.
- Explain the difference(s) between the Thinking and Feeling Preferences.
- Define *introvert* and *extrovert*.
- Explain the difference(s) between the Judging and Perceiving Orientations.
- Name the psychologist who designed the Personality Assessment System (PAS).
- According to the PAS, what are the three major dimensions of personality functioning?
- Explain the difference(s) between a Cognitive Externalizer and Internalizer.
- Explain the difference(s) between an Emotional Role-Regulated person and a Role-Flexible person.
- Explain the difference(s) between a Social Role-Adapted person and a Role-Regulated person.
- Describe your personality using the Myers-Briggs typology.
- Describe your personality using PAS dimensions.

TOPIC SCENARIO

Nigel and Jeremy recently turned 30 and have been best friends since they were kids. Besides Jeremy, Nigel has a large circle of friends and is extremely outgoing. Jeremy prefers to spend time alone or in the company of a few close friends. In high school, Nigel played soccer and joined the debate team. Meanwhile, Jeremy played guitar and drew comics. Nigel enjoys interaction and has worked in the fields of sales and customer service. Jeremy enjoys art and technology and has been working as a Web designer. Nigel sometimes gets the pair into trouble for acting before thinking, and Jeremy comes up with creative solutions to solve their problems. Both friends have enrolled in an online college and are seeking to further their careers by getting degrees. Jeremy wonders if he has the discipline to study and excel with no teachers or other students around. Nigel wonders if he has the organizational skills to balance work and school.

Based on Nigel's and Jeremy's situations, answer the following questions:

▶ Think about your own personality. Do you find you "relate" more closely to Nigel or to Jeremy?

Image copyright Junial Enterprises, 2009. Used under license from shutterstock.com

- ❯ What are some words you would use to describe Nigel's personality?
- ❯ What are some words you would use to describe Jeremy's personality?
- ❯ In what ways could Nigel's personality influence his learning style?
- ❯ In what ways could Jeremy's personality influence his learning style?

❝ *I want all my senses engaged. Let me absorb the world's variety and uniqueness.*

—Maya Angelou,
Grammy award-winning author (best spoken word)
and Pulitzer Prize nominee

4

SUCCESS: A PERSONALIZED PATH

Image copyright shae cardenas, 2009. Used under license from shutterstock.com

These days, business tycoons, major league athletes, and movie stars are all celebrities alike. We look at their success with glassy eyes and want to be just like them. This misstep in thinking starts us on the wrong course. We don't achieve success by denying who we are or by becoming who we aren't. We get there by analyzing ourselves and knowing what makes us stand out as special. When we know who we are and where we are strong, we can begin the process of developing our talents and targeting success.

Many elements of our society reward us for conforming. In an attempt to "fit in," we take on the appearance, the language and the behavior of others. Although this provides us with a sense of belonging, important elements of our personal identity are sacrificed.

The key to success is learning how to best operate within a master group or culture (school, home, work) while maintaining and developing those qualities that make you most special.

❯ REFLECTION QUESTIONS

- Think of a couple of successful people you admire. What positive traits do they have that make them unique?
- What positive traits do you have that make you unique?

Apply **It!**

Your Uniqueness Factor

Goal: To create a list of qualities and strengths that make you stand out.

STEP 1: Think about activities that you do with ease. These are things that are comfortable for you because you have natural abilities or you have developed strengths.

STEP 2: Think about attributes that other people have complimented you on. These can be qualities such as a photographic memory, encyclopedic knowledge, or incredible sense of humor.

STEP 3: Think about positive adjectives you would use to distinguish yourself when replying to a classified ad for a job or a date. Keep it clean!

STEP 4: Record your thoughts and observations in a journal or Word document.

PERSONALITY, LEARNING, AND YOU

Merriam Webster defines personality as: "the collection of emotional and behavioral traits that characterize a person." Your personality drives both your responses and your actions. That is why it is important for you to develop a full understanding of your own personality. By isolating components of your personality, you can actively work to harness your strengths and to develop more qualities you value.

Insight into your personality provides clues to your preferred learning style (see Chapter 5). There are many different ways of absorbing information; with no particular learning style being the "right one." When you assess your personality, you will know which learning styles are right for you as an individual.

PERSONALITY TYPE

Acquiring perspective of your own personality helps you to understand the reasons behind why you think as you do, feel as you do, and do what you do. When you gain more self-understanding, you increase your ability for self-determination. Then you can apply your understanding of personality differences to interactions with others. Your new insights will enable you to more positively and powerfully relate.

The Myers-Briggs Type Indicator® is a personality type assessment system created by Katharine Briggs and Isabel Briggs Myers, based on the ideas and theories of psychologist Carl Jung.

REFLECTION QUESTIONS

- What are five words other people have used to describe you?
- What are five words you would use to describe yourself?

Apply **It!**

Carl Jung: Founder of Analytical Psychology

Goal: To get an introduction to Carl Jung, on whose ideas the Myers-Briggs Type Indicator® (discussed in this chapter) is based.

STEP 1: Conduct a Web search for articles on Carl Jung.

STEP 2: Find a Web site that you consider credible and that contains an article that has useful introductory information on Carl Jung.

STEP 3: Read the article. Were you familiar with any of Jung's ideas from popular culture or under different names?

Image copyright Le Loft 1911, 2009. Used under license from shutterstock.com

MENTAL PROCESSES AND ORIENTATIONS

The Briggs and Myers mother/daughter team concluded that human beings differ from one another in four primary ways, or preferences. These preferences combined form a personality type. Briggs and Myers likened their system of preferences to the ability to use our hands: most of us can use both hands but have a preference (innate, learned, or chosen) for one over the other. Similarly, although a spectrum of personality types exists, we each have a preference, or type, that influences how we interact with the world around us. Knowing your type will shed light on your uniqueness factor and help identify the best ways for you to learn.

Perceiving

The first set of mental preferences in the Myers-Briggs Type Indicator® relates to how people "perceive" or take in information. If you

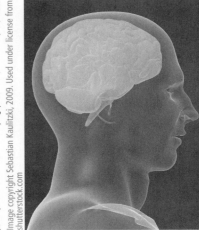

Image copyright Sebastian Kaulitzki, 2009. Used under license from shutterstock.com

prefer the Sensing Perception, you like facts and data that exist in the here and now. The Sensing side of our brain is rooted in the present day reality of our surroundings. It notices, organizes, and remembers the sights, sounds, and smells of our daily existences. For example, an online learner with the Sensing Preference recalls her daily spending and enters the data in a budget spreadsheet.

If you prefer the Intuition Perception, you like information that is more abstract and represents imaginative possibilities for the future. The Intuitive side of our brain interprets "big-picture" patterns of all the information we take in and forms impressions and theories. It speculates on future possibilities. For example, an online learner with an Intuition Preference reviews a year's worth of trends on diet and exercise habits and interprets how it forms the bigger picture of his health.

SENSING PREFERENCE VS. INTUITION PREFERENCE

If You Are a Sense Perceptive:	If You Are an Intuitive Perceptive:
• You live in the now and embrace the present.	• You contemplate the future and look forward to future possibilities.
• You apply common sense to problem solving.	• You apply creativity to problem solving.
• You have a good memory for statistics.	• You have a good memory for context.
• You act on experience.	• You act on theory.
• You require clarity.	• You are comfortable with ambiguity.

Judging

The second set of mental preferences identifies how people form "judgments" or make decisions. If you prefer the Thinking Judgment, you tend to make decisions in an analytical manner with an emphasis on results. The Thinking side of our brains analyzes information objectively and forms logical conclusions from a detached perspective. For example, an online learner using the Thinking Judgment may choose to take a particular online class because it is a core requirement in a degree program.

If you prefer the Feeling Judgment, you make your decisions in a holistic way, emphasizing the importance of the whole and the interdependence of its parts. The Feeling side of our brain is subjective; it forms conclusions in an attached manner based on likes/dislikes, impact on others, and personal values. For example, an online learner using the Feeling Judgment may choose to take a particular online class based on the opinions of friends.

Image copyright Coka, 2009. Used under license from shutterstock.com

THINKING PREFERENCE VS. FEELING PREFERENCE

If You Make Judgments by Thinking:	**If You Make Judgments by Feeling:**
• You use objective analysis.	• You use subjective measures.
• You naturally notice work to be accomplished.	• You are naturally sensitive to peoples' needs.
• You make decisions using logic.	• You make decisions using personal feelings.
• You accept conflict.	• You are unsettled by conflict.

Introversion and Extraversion

The dimension of personality discovered by Carl Jung is called Extraversion-Introversion. If you prefer Introversion, you are introspective and draw your primary energy from the inner world of information, thoughts, ideas, and other reflections. An introvert could be found listening to music and writing poetry in a journal under a tree. If you prefer Extraversion, you like to engage with the outside world as your prime life force. An extrovert could be found at an Open Mic or Poetry Slam debuting poetry in front of an audience.

Online learning has great ways for both introverts and extroverts to communicate. An introvert typically prefers to think something through and then send it to the instructor or classmates by e-mail. The introvert also likes the intimate one-on-one dialogue of an instant message session. Extroverts can be found in chat rooms, posting on bulletin boards, and social networking to make friends to connect with both online and offline.

4

Image copyright digitalskillet, 2009. Used under license from shutterstock.com

REFLECTION QUESTIONS

- Have you ever felt like you have to "get away from it all" to "recharge your batteries"? What led up to that feeling, and what did you do about it?
- Do you ever feel like you're missing out when you spend time alone?

INTROVERTS VS. EXTROVERTS

As an Introvert:

- You think before acting.
- You prefer intimate relationships.
- You require alone time.
- You are motivated by your own thoughts and ideas.

As an Extrovert:

- You act before thinking.
- You enjoy group activities.
- You dislike being alone.
- You are motivated by people and energized by activity.

Action Orientation

The final dimension of personality in the Myers-Briggs typology is the style you use to interact with the outside world: Judging or Perceiving. We all use both judging and perceiving processes to store information, organize thoughts, make decisions, take actions, and manage our lives. Yet one of these processes tends to take the lead in our relationship with the outside world, while the other governs our inner world.

If you have a Judging Orientation, you have a planned approach to the outside world. You rely on your Thinking or Feeling preference to manage your outer life. Your friends and coworkers may call you a planner, and your drive is to organize the outside world.

Online learners of the Judging Orientation typically plan their college experience from start to finish with the end result of a career in mind.

If you have a Perceiving Orientation, you take the outside world as it comes. You rely on your Sensing or Intuition preference to run your outer life. Your friends and coworkers refer to you as flexible, and your drive is to experience the outside world and stay open to its many possibilities.

Online learners of the Perceiving Orientation have a more fluid approach to their education and adapt their academic and career goals as they go.

Image copyright IKO, 2009. Used under license from shutterstock.com

---

JUDGING ORIENTATION VS. PERCEIVING ORIENTATION

If You Have a Judging Orientation:	**If You Have a Perceiving Orientation:**
• You are a planner.	• You develop strategy as you go.
• You prefer routines.	• You prefer variety flexibility.
• You like to complete a single task before moving on to another.	• You are good at multitasking.
• You avoid stress by staying ahead of deadlines.	• You work best close to deadlines.

Apply **It!**

Five Tests You Will Actually Enjoy Taking

GOAL: To learn more about your personality type.

STEP 1: Identify your personal type in the Jung Typology Test at http://www.humanmetrics.com/.

STEP 2: Take this psychology test to find out more about your personality: http://www.outofservice.com/bigfive.

STEP 3: Are you a visual learner? Take a short quiz modeled as a graphical presentation of both Keirsey's Temperament and the Myers-Briggs Type Indicator® at http://www.truecolorscareer.com.

STEP 4: By now, you should know a lot about yourself. Choose a personality test of your own here: http://similarminds.com/.

STEP 5: You're almost finished, so here's a treat: Edy's Grand Ice Cream commissioned a study into the link between personality and ice cream flavor preference. You can test your ice cream preference here and sample from an assortment of other quizzes that put the "personality" back in "personality test": http://www.personalityquiz.net/.

REFLECTION QUESTIONS

- When you take a trip or vacation, do you prefer to plan it out in advance or to see where the day takes you?
- How do you feel about the following statement: "I leave work until the last minute because I am motivated by the challenge of a tight deadline."

PERSONALITY DEVELOPMENT

Because your personality is multifaceted, there are also many approaches to assessing it. The Personality Assessment System (PAS) is one of the most complex, yet practical, theories of personality development in existence today. Dr. John William Gittinger, an Oklahoma psychologist, studied groups of personality traits that developed over time and called them *dimensions*.

These dimensions affect how and what we learn and how we respond to the world around us. The people we like, the subjects we enjoy, the way we learn, and the careers we choose are all affected by our personality dimensional makeup.

According to Gittinger, the three major dimensions of personality functioning are the cognitive dimension, the emotional dimension, and the social dimension.

THE COGNITIVE DIMENSION

The cognitive dimension deals with ideas and how we perceive things. This dimension defines the quality and content of our mental activity. Within the cognitive dimension, there is an Externalizer and an Internalizer.

The Cognitive Externalizer is naturally in touch with the surroundings and directly relates to people and things. The Externalizer is mentally involved with what is reached through the senses. Externalizers prefer doing things more than thinking about them.

For example, an online learner who is a Cognitive Externalizer gathers research for a psychology project by conducting "man-on-the-street" interviews or a focus group where there is opportunity to interact with other people.

The Cognitive Internalizer is naturally in touch with the inner self. Internalizers are involved with abstract ideas and withdraw when interaction with people becomes more intrusive than enjoyable. Internalizers relate to others when the interaction supports internal needs.

For example, an online learner who is a Cognitive Internalizer researches a psychology project by searching the Web to read about prior studies and opposing theories.

Image copyright Lisa F. Young, 2009. Used under license from shutterstock.com

4

THE COGNITIVE/INTELLECTUAL DIMENSION

If You Are an Externalizer:

- You respond to external cues.
- You are people-oriented and have many acquaintances and friends.
- You engage physically.
- You enjoy "doing."
- You are reenergized by activity with others.

If You Are an Internalizer:

- You respond to internal cues.
- You are people-oriented and have a small group of close-knit friends.
- You engage mentally.
- You enjoy "thinking."
- You are reenergized by private time after activity with others.

▶ REFLECTION QUESTIONS

- How do you feel about working on group projects?
- With your own work, do you prefer to think things out or plunge right in?

THE EMOTIONAL DIMENSION

The emotional dimension deals with, you guessed it, emotions. It also affects how we approach tasks. Because of this, the emotional dimension is sometimes called the procedural dimension.

The Emotional Role-Regulated person is naturally organized and precise. Regulated people use logic and step-by-step methods to approach tasks. Regulated individuals are detail-oriented and separate thoughts from action to focus on the specifics.

For example, an Emotional Role-Regulated online learner who has several deadlines coming up this week prepares a step-by-step plan to accomplish everything on her agenda.

The Emotional Role-Flexible person is naturally spontaneous. Flexible people use trial and error methods to approach tasks. Flexible people are broad thinkers and focus on concepts and possibilities.

For example, an Emotional Role-Flexible online learner who has several deadlines coming up this week starts one project and works on it for a while, and then moves onto another until eventually all work is complete.

THE EMOTIONAL/PROCEDURAL DIMENSION

If You Are Flexible:

- You are sensitive.
- You are insightful.
- You are empathic.
- You are concept-oriented.
- You have a variable style of concentration.

If You Are Regulated:

- You are objective.
- You are logical.
- You are procedural.
- You are structured in your orientation.
- You have a focused style of concentration.

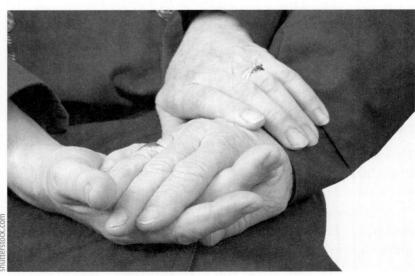

THE SOCIAL DIMENSION

The social dimension deals with interpersonal style and skill. It describes how we respond to social cues and how readily our behavior adapts to social demands.

The Social Role-uniform person prefers to socialize in small groups of like-minded people. These people are more set in the way they approach social situations, and they choose environments where their interests are similar to others.

For example, a Social Role-uniform online learner takes his mentor's advice to get involved in his school's community. He chooses to join a student political group with which he already is affiliated outside of school.

The Social Role-adaptive person moves in and out of different social groups with ease. Role-adaptive people have the ability to quickly assess the demands of the environment and act accordingly. They are comfortable operating in many different kinds of environments.

For example, a Social Role-uniform online learner takes her mentor's advice to get involved in her school's community. She chooses to join the school's online newspaper, a chat group for mothers, and a weekly online gaming competition.

THE SOCIAL DIMENSION

If You Are Adaptable:

- You generate a good first impression.

- You are socially comfortable in varied settings.

- You can change social roles with ease.

If You Are Role Uniform:

- You generate best impressions with like-minded people.

- You are most socially comfortable with familiar settings.

- You have an established social role and like it that way.

▶ REFLECTION QUESTIONS

- How do you feel in groups of people that include people who are very different from you?
- Do you think you can learn things from people with opposing viewpoints and values?

4

CHAPTER SUMMARY

Success is not achieved by following in the paths of others. We get there by looking inward and knowing what makes us special. This chapter provided you with tools to analyze your personality and learning style(s). As you saw, there is not one template for success but several possible combinations and clusters. By knowing where you fall on a spectrum of personality types, you can adapt your habits to highlight your skills and work on your deficiencies. This insight can have a powerful impact on your education, career, and life.

POINTS TO KEEP IN MIND

In this chapter, several main points were discussed in detail:

▶ The key to success is learning how to best operate within a master group or culture (school, home, work) while maintaining and developing those qualities that make you most special.

▶ By analyzing your personality, you can actively work to harness your strengths and to develop additional qualities you value.

▶ The Myers-Briggs Type Indicator® is a personality type assessment system with 16 combinations created by Katharine Briggs and Isabel Briggs Myers and is based on the theories of psychologist Carl Jung.

Image copyright Chad McDermott, 2009. Used under license from shutterstock.com

▶ The Personality Assessment System (PAS) identifies three major dimensions of personality functioning that evolve and develop over time: the cognitive dimension, the emotional dimension, and the social dimension.

▶ Knowing about your personality highlights your uniqueness factor and helps identify the best ways for you to grow and learn.

LEARNING OBJECTIVES REVISITED

Review the learning objectives for this chapter, and rate your level of achievement for each objective using the rating scale provided. For each objective on which you do not rate yourself as a 3, outline a plan of action that you will take to fully achieve the objective. Include a time frame for this plan.

1 = did not successfully achieve objective

2 = understand what is needed, but need more study or practice

3 = achieved learning objective thoroughly

4

	1	2	3
Provide a definition for *personality*.	☐	☐	☐
Name the system for identifying different personality types based on the theories of Carl Jung.	☐	☐	☐
Explain the difference(s) between the Sensing and Intuition Preferences.	☐	☐	☐
Explain the difference(s) between the Thinking and Feeling Preferences.	☐	☐	☐
Define *introvert* and *extrovert*.	☐	☐	☐
Explain the difference(s) between the Judging and Perceiving Orientations.	☐	☐	☐
Name the psychologist who designed the Personality Assessment System (PAS).	☐	☐	☐
According to the PAS, what are the three major dimensions of personality functioning?	☐	☐	☐
Explain the difference(s) between a Cognitive Externalizer and a Cognitive Internalizer.	☐	☐	☐
Explain the difference(s) between an Emotional Role-Regulated person and a Role-Flexible person.	☐	☐	☐
Explain the difference(s) between a Social Role-Adapted person and a Role-Regulated person.	☐	☐	☐
Describe your personality using the Myers-Briggs typology.	☐	☐	☐
Describe your personality using PAS dimensions.	☐	☐	☐

Steps to Achieve Unmet Objectives

Steps   Due Date

1. _____   _____

2. _____   _____

3. _____   _____

4. _____   _____

5. _____   _____

6. _____   _____

7. _____   _____

REFERENCES

Briggs Myers & Briggs Myers. (1995). *Gifts differing: Understanding personality types.* Davies-Black Publishing.

Downing, S. (2005). *On course strategies for creating success in college and in life (4th ed.).* Houghton Mifflin Company.

DuVivier, R. S. (2005). *Your strategic future: developing a career path to success.* Thomson-Delmar Learning.

Gittinger, J. W. The Personality Assessment System (PAS). Retrieved from http://www.pasf.org/summary.htm

Guilbert, S. D. (2001). *How to be a successful online student.* McGraw-Hill.

Krauskopf, & Saunders. Career assessment with the personality assessment system. Retrieved from *Sage Journals Online:* http://jca.sagepub.com/cgi/content/abstract/3/3/241

Leshin, C. B. (1998). Student resource guide to the Internet, student success online. Prentice Hall.

Reinhold, R. Personality pathways exploring personality type and its applications. What is your Myers Briggs Personality. Retrieved from http://www.personalitypathways.com/type_inventory.html

Saunders, D. Former Head of Personality Research at ETS, Chapel Hill, NC.

Soundview Editorial Staff. (1989). Skills for success, the experts show the way.

Wahlstrom, Williams, & Shea. (2003). *The successful distance learning student.* Wadsworth/Thomson Learning.

White & Baker. (2004). *The student guide to successful online learning.* Pearson Education, Inc.

4

CHAPTER OUTLINE

The Virtual Classroom

Learning Styles

Learning Environments

5 The Virtual Classroom

LEARNING OBJECTIVES

CHAPTER

10
9
8
7
6
5
4
3
2
1

By the end of this chapter, students should have achieved the following objectives:

▶ Identify the psychologist who came up with the nine major reference groups for learning styles.
▶ List an advantage of the Rule-Enhanced Learner Style.
▶ List an advantage of the Structurally-Enhanced Learner Style.
▶ List an advantage of the Interpersonally-Enhanced Learner Style.
▶ List an advantage of the Supportive Learner Style.
▶ List an advantage of the Idealistic Learner Style.
▶ List an advantage of the Individualistic Learner Style.
▶ List an advantage of the Learning Leader Style.
▶ List an advantage of the Organizing Learner Style.
▶ List an advantage of the Controlling Learner Style.
▶ List three qualities of an externalized learning environment.
▶ List three qualities of an internalized learning environment.
▶ List three qualities of a regulated learning environment.
▶ List three qualities of a flexible learning environment.

● TOPIC SCENARIO

Heather has been attending an online aviation school for three months. She consistently got good grades, especially doing lab sciences, in high school, but she is already struggling to keep up. She has always liked working on cars and is employed part time at an auto body shop. She likes when she can apprentice one of the mechanics on a tough job. A good day for Heather is one in which she comes home covered in grease and oil.

Heather wonders if maybe that is the problem. Although she knows that she has to study, she wishes the online school she chose offered more than just the minimum required hands-on fieldwork. Her instructors aren't around much and assign large chunks of text to read with frequent multiple-choice quizzes. Heather has never been great with memorizing words, but she can point out the parts of an engine if she just has one to look at. She knows in order to get a better job working on planes she has to get certified.

Based on Heather's situation, answer the following questions:

▶ In what types of learning situations does Heather appear to do well?

▶ In what types of learning situations does Heather appear to do poorly?

▶ In what ways do you think it is possible to get a hands-on education at an online college?

▶ How can understanding your own learning preferences contribute to your success at an online college?

▶ What part does the online college you choose play in your outcome for success?

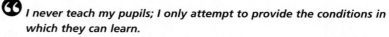 *I never teach my pupils; I only attempt to provide the conditions in which they can learn.*

—Albert Einstein,
Nobel Prize-winning physicist

THE VIRTUAL CLASSROOM

You don't fit in a box and neither does your education. Online education opens doors, literally, figuratively, and virtually. Online education is not just about you and your computer. Introverts and extroverts (see Chapter 3) have different needs. The virtual classroom provides interaction on the levels you choose (see Chapter 2). There are online universities where you can select from a preestablished program or creatively build your own degree. Your virtual classroom is open at morning, noon, and night; it accommodates morning people and night owls alike. Now that you have some insight into your personality type, let's take a look at *learning styles* and *learning environments*.

REFLECTION QUESTIONS

- In what classroom activities are you most comfortable?
- What are some types of traditional classroom activities you think you would miss with online education? How might you re-create these activities in the virtual classroom?

5

LEARNING STYLES

Yes, it's true that each of us is unique. But we are part of larger groups of learners when it comes to studying online. David Saunders, a well-known research psychologist, worked for many decades to cluster personality patterns into groups of people with similar traits. His work resulted in the formation of nine major reference groups that describe much of the fundamental differences among us:

1. Rule-Enhanced Learner
2. Structurally-Enhanced Learner
3. Interpersonally-Enhanced Learner
4. Supportive Learner
5. Idealistic Learner
6. Individualistic Learner
7. Learning Leader
8. Organizing Learner
9. Controlling Learner

Read about Saunders' nine styles of online learning. Think about the learning styles that describe you and which styles are most different.

THE RULE-ENHANCED LEARNER

You prefer rules and orderliness. Your learning is enhanced by structure. Clear expectations and assignments with deadlines help you to function more comfortably and successfully.

Rule-Enhanced Learner Advantages

1. You enjoy working on your own. You will have many opportunities to work independently as an online learner.

2. You like to pursue your special interests. They really capture your attention. You will enjoy online projects.

3. You prefer periodic, focused communication when interacting with fellow students and teachers. Your interactions in discussion groups and interviews will be productive and purpose driven.

4. Online learning is structured and provides clear assignments in the form of learning activities. You are good at understanding rules and following them. The format of online learning will be comfortable for you.

5. You have effective study skills and habits, which are key ingredients to success in online learning.

Image copyright Dash, 2009. Used under license from shutterstock.com

Image copyright Edyta Pawlowska, 2009. Used under license from shutterstock.com

5

THE STRUCTURALLY-ENHANCED LEARNER

You learn best when structure is provided. You follow direction and expect it to be provided. Your experience is enhanced when someone helps you to structure your time and your learning activities.

Structurally-Enhanced Learner Advantages

1. You learn by doing things. You will enjoy the learning activities involved in online education that get you in touch with the real world. Activities such as "interviews" and "guided laboratory practice" will be of special interest to you.

2. You respond well to direction and guidance. You perform best when you receive oversight, direction, and support.

THE INTERPERSONALLY-ENHANCED LEARNER

You often find yourself the center of attention. People provide you stimulation and affirmation. You respond well to the spotlight. Your experience is enhanced greatly by reinforcement from others. You learn best when you can be expressive and receive recognition for your talent.

Image copyright Yuri Arcurs, 2009. Used under license from shutterstock.com

5

▶ REFLECTION QUESTIONS

- Which learning style groups work best on their own?
- Which learning style groups most need interaction with faculty and peer groups?

Image copyright Yuri Arcurs, 2009. Used under license from shutterstock.com

Interpersonally-Enhanced Learner Advantages

1. You are confident in your skills to succeed in any educational environment. Online education poses a new challenge, one that you expect to navigate well.

2. You have the ability to cope with whatever life throws at you. You have a good track record of success. The online environment will present opportunities to demonstrate your skills.

3. You are expressive. Online learning provides chats and discussion groups as forums for e-dialogue as well as critiques, interview documentation, and research papers as forums for written expression.

THE SUPPORTIVE LEARNER

You are a people person. You recognize peoples' needs and know how to be of help. You learn best when you can relate to others and understand their needs and interests. You prefer learning activities where you can exercise your skill in helping others.

Supportive Learner Advantages

1. You plan ahead. Planning and preparation are the keys to success in online learning.

2. You know your strengths and make allowances for your limitations to stay ahead.

3. You are especially skillful in professional coursework focusing on "caring for others." You are supportive, involved, and motivated by the opportunity to "serve."

THE IDEALISTIC LEARNER

You have high ideals and choose to be involved in projects and programs that "matter." Your insights help you to design activities that make a difference. You are stimulated by opportunities to make improvements in the world around you. You learn best in programs that provide these avenues to you.

Idealist Learner Advantages

1. You have inherent talent and skills. This talent and skill set gives you the confidence to undertake online learning.

5

Should you lack some skills for online learning, you have the aptitude to successfully acquire them.

2. You have a sense of mission and priorities. You have selected online learning as the best plan for you, and you have the motivation to achieve your goals.

3. You are naturally organized. This trait will help you to build a realistic schedule to complete course-specific learning activities.

4. You are motivated to improve things and make systems more effective. You will enjoy content that is thought provoking and gets your idealistic ideas flowing. You may even find ways to improve online learning for the benefit of your class.

5. You plan ahead. Planning and preparation are the keys to success in online learning.

6. You know your strengths and make allowances for your limitations to stay ahead.

THE INDIVIDUALISTIC LEARNER

You are an individualist. You have the confidence and comfort to work independently toward your goals. You really focus on your interests and explore them in detail. You learn well in educationally enriching environments.

Individualist Learner Advantages

1. You are very comfortable working alone. This ability to function independently is important for success in online learning.

2. You have special interests that really capture your attention. You will be able to focus well on your distance education program.

3. You are a self-starter. This trait will help you to organize learning activities on your own to get things done.

4. You have good research skills. All online programs require research activity. You are well suited to online research and investigation.

5. You have natural talent in technical matters. Online course-work requires strong technical skills. You have a natural aptitude to acquire technical understanding and skills important for success in online learning.

6. You don't need much direction or supervision. Distance learners are expected to work relatively independently on their coursework, and clearly you can. That is an important predictor for online success.

7. You are focused, you plan ahead, and you prepare effectively. Those skills are important in organizing and prioritizing online learning assignments.

8. You have clearly defined strengths in specialty areas. You are most satisfied if your online program matches your specialty interests.

THE LEARNING LEADER

You like to assume responsibility. You take charge of others comfortably. You really know how to organize people to achieve a goal! You learn best in programs where you can have opportunities to direct others and get things done.

Image copyright Stephen Coburn, 2009. Used under license from shutterstock.com

Learning Leader Advantages

1. You are an independent learner. This is perhaps the most important quality in successful online learning. The distance environment requires that you be comfortable structuring your time and working independently. This seems to be easy for you.

2. You like to take responsibility and take charge. You will have many opportunities to assume responsibility for yourself and small groups in the online environment. You will be comfortable organizing yourself and others to get your online tasks done.

3. You like to relate to people but don't become involved. Online learning provides many opportunities to discuss, debate, and question peers on academic topics. You will welcome peer review and feedback to assist you in pursuit of your career goals.

4. You are good at acquiring knowledge. This is an excellent skill for success in online learning. You will be exposed to

5

many learning modalities (lecture, discussion, chats, field-work). You will have many varied opportunities to increase your knowledge through online education.

THE ORGANIZING LEARNER

You like to make order out of chaos. You see how things can be organized effectively. You really manage tasks well and accomplish a lot in a short amount of time. You like to have the opportunity to show your skills and their value to others. You learn best in situations where you can apply your organizational skills in a practical way.

Organizing Learner Advantages

1. You have natural skills and talents that will help you in online learning. You have good academic discipline and have had success in other academic pursuits. This makes success in online learning a strong likelihood.

2. You are really organized. Strong organizational skills are necessary to keep yourself on track with online learning activities. You are accustomed to balancing work and like responsibilities effectively. Online learning can be effectively integrated into your priorities.

Image copyright Kiselev Andrey Valerevich, 2009. Used under license from shutterstock.com

3. You have the ability to draw upon all your resources in pursuit of a goal. You are a good multitasker. The most effective online learners are excellent at prioritizing and multitasking.

THE CONTROLLING LEARNER

You like to be in control. You are interested in details and managing them effectively. Controlling outcomes matters to you. You learn best in structured situations where clear direction is provided.

Controlling Learner Advantages

1. You want to be a part of the solution. You are driven to become involved so you can improve things and make them better. You will enjoy online classes that give you the opportunity to analyze and develop systems to improve current practices.
2. You are conscientious. If you have responsibility, you take it seriously and deliver. You like order and can create it if no structure exists. You have the ability to structure online activities.

REFLECTION QUESTIONS

- What is your preferred learning style?
- What are the advantages to your style for online learning?
- What aspects of the other learning styles do you think you should adopt to increase your versatility and accomplish your goals?

5

Image copyright Andrew Gentry, 2009. Used under license from shutterstock.com

Apply **It!**

Understanding People Who Are Different

Goal: To enhance your understanding of different types of learners.

STEP 1: Refresh your knowledge of the nine different learning styles.

STEP 2: Over the course of a week or so, keep the nine learning styles in your mind as you interact with friends, family, and coworkers.

STEP 3: Try to identify a representative from all nine learning styles. Feel free to discuss Saunders' research out loud. The members of your social circle may be as interested as you.

LEARNING ENVIRONMENTS

At this point, you understand how your personality affects your learning style. Now, let's talk about coordinating your personality and learning style with the appropriate learning environment. Finding the right learning environment is as important as choosing a field of study. In the right environment, a student can flourish. Remember Katharine Briggs and Isabel Briggs Myers and Dr. John Gittinger from Chapter 3? Their theories on personality type and assessment will come in handy as you match your personality type and preferred learning style to a corresponding learning environment.

THE EXTERNALIZED LEARNING ENVIRONMENT

The externalized learning environment is a place to interact with people and things. It is action-oriented, and activities are practical, tangible, and realistic. "E" environments feature visual tools, demonstrations, and hands-on experience.

Opportunities for dialogue and discussion are plentiful in the E environment, as E students like to talk through their information processing. E students are environmentally alert and are energized by a class with meaning and purpose. Engaging by participating meets the needs of functional E students.

Image copyright Yuri Arcurs, 2009. Used under license from shutterstock.com

Qualities of Externalized Learning Environments

▶ Experimental learning

▶ Group discussion

▶ Charts, graphs, diagrams, visual aids

▶ Group projects

▶ Hands-on experience

▶ Laboratory experience

▶ Field study

▶ Role play

E's may need to make adaptations to the online learning environment to engage in these activities. Advances in technology have enabled people in different locations to communicate in real time while seeing and hearing each other.

THE INTERNALIZED LEARNING ENVIRONMENT

The internalized learning environment emphasizes private time for thinking. It supports the generation of concepts and ideas. The "I" environment provides time to be spent in the inner world of thought. Reading, watching instructional media productions, and listening to lectures are examples of learning activities in I environments.

Image copyright Jaimie Duplass, 2009. Used under license from shutterstock.com

5

I environments balance private contemplation time and activities designed to stimulate. Being comfortable in their inner landscape, I students may be prone to distractions or daydreaming as a form of mental retreat. In successful I environments, thinking time is followed by activity. This teaches I learners discipline and realistic follow-through.

Qualities of Internalized Learning Environments

- Reading
- Lectures/videoconferencing
- Audio lessons
- Independent learning or self-directed learning
- Individualized study
- Writing activities such as journaling or Web logging (blogging)
- Group activities where students privately create ideas and share them with the group

THE REGULATED LEARNING ENVIRONMENT

The regulated learning environment is a structured environment. A step-by-step approach to teaching benefits learners in the "R"

▶ REFLECTION QUESTION

- Think about classes you've liked and disliked in the past. How can an improved understanding of yourself help you make better choices in your online program of study?

Image copyright Lee Morris, 2009. Used under license from shutterstock.com

environment. R learners appreciate facts, details, and logic. Drills and memorization are examples of learning activities in the R environment.

The R learning situation is characterized by the presence of order and organization. Communication between the students and the instructors is clear and direct.

Qualities of Regulated Learning Environments

▶ Memorization

▶ Drill

▶ Step-by-step approaches

▶ Numbering concept

▶ Outlining

▶ Programmed, sequenced instruction

▶ Focus on detail

▶ Attention to precision, accuracy, logic

THE FLEXIBLE LEARNING ENVIRONMENT

The flexible learning environment gives you room to express yourself as an individual. Creative activity and originality are encouraged. The flexible environment recognizes student empathy, sensitivities, and insight. "F" learners prefer to grasp the essence of issues rather than details or isolated facts. In the flexible learning environment, students learn through experience and move through learning activities in an exploratory, trial-and-error fashion.

The flexible learning environment rewards insightful problem solving. The F environment supports F students by providing an understanding of the whole concept, idea, project, or task before reporting the details.

Qualities of Flexible Learning Environments

- ◗ Trial-and-error learning.
- ◗ Experimental learning.
- ◗ Explain "why," before "how/when" teaching.
- ◗ Facilitate creative expression and original idea generation.
- ◗ Loose organization and control from instructor.
- ◗ Content should engage the emotions.
- ◗ Allow for spontaneity of interest. Permit time to explore topics/issues that arise naturally in the course of discussion.

 Apply **It!**

Online College Learning Environments

Goal: To identify different learning environments in online education.

STEP 1: Conduct a Web search for online colleges. Your search may lead you directly to an online college, a directory of online colleges, or a Web site about online colleges.

STEP 2: Choose four online colleges, and read briefly about their curriculum and style.

STEP 3: Can you tell whether these colleges would be externalized, internalized, regulated, or flexible learning environments? Write down the names of the colleges followed by observations supporting your conclusions.

CHAPTER SUMMARY

When you take classes online, you are choosing to study in an electronic environment. This setting is really the sum total of a cluster of smaller learning environments. To be successful in these learning methods, you must first understand your usual response to them by assessing your learning style. After you know your preferred learning style, you will be able to better choose the type of electronic environment that will work for you.

POINTS TO KEEP IN MIND

In this chapter, several main points were discussed in detail:

▶ Psychologist David Saunders identified nine different styles of learning, each with its own advantages. There is no one best learning style.

▶ The key to finding your preferred learning style is in understanding your personality. After you know which learning style works best for you, you should remain open to the other styles to be versatile.

▶ Finding the right learning environment is as important as choosing a field of study. In the right environment, a student can flourish.

▶ Knowing the qualities of the four different learning environments will help you decide if your personality and learning style are good matches for the environment.

LEARNING OBJECTIVES REVISITED

Review the learning objectives for this chapter, and rate your level of achievement for each objective using the rating scale provided. For each objective on which you do not rate yourself as a 3, outline a plan of action that you will take to fully achieve the objective. Include a time frame for this plan.

1 = did not successfully achieve objective

2 = understand what is needed, but need more study or practice

3 = achieved learning objective thoroughly

	1	2	3
Identify the psychologist who came up with the nine major reference groups for learning styles.	☐	☐	☐
List an advantage of the Rule-Enhanced Learner Style.	☐	☐	☐
List an advantage of the Structurally-Enhanced Learner Style.	☐	☐	☐
List an advantage of the Interpersonally-Enhanced Learner Style.	☐	☐	☐
List an advantage of the Supportive Learner Style.	☐	☐	☐
List an advantage of the Idealistic Learner Style.	☐	☐	☐
List an advantage of the Individualistic Learner Style.	☐	☐	☐
List an advantage of the Learning Leader Style.	☐	☐	☐
List an advantage of the Organizing Learner Style.	☐	☐	☐
List an advantage of the Controlling Learner Style.	☐	☐	☐
List three qualities of an externalized learning environment.	☐	☐	☐
List three qualities of an internalized learning environment.	☐	☐	☐
List three qualities of a regulated learning environment.	☐	☐	☐
List three qualities of a flexible learning environment.	☐	☐	☐

Steps to Achieve Unmet Objectives

Steps   Due Date

1. _____   _____

2. _____   _____

3. _____   _____

4. _____   _____

5. _____   _____

6. _____   _____

7. _____   _____

REFERENCES

DuVivier, R. S. (1992). *Diagnosis and treatment in education, a handbook for applying the impressionistic models system in teaching and student development.* University Press of America.

Krauskopf, and Saunders. Career assessment with the personality assessment system. Retrieved from *Sage Journals Online:* http://jca.sagepub.com/cgi/content/abstract/3/3/241

Krauskopf & Saunders. (1994). *Personality and ability: The personality assessment system.* Rowman & Littlefield Pub Group.

Maiden, B. ASTD's source for e-learning, virtual classroom starter guide. Retrieved from http://www.learningcircuits.org/2003/oct2003/maiden.htm

Reference Groups: A view taking of the, David R. Saunders, MARS Measurement Associates, 1985 - presented at the annual meeting of the PAS Foundation. Unpublished document from the PAS archives.

5

CHAPTER OUTLINE

6 Learning Strategies

LEARNING OBJECTIVES

CHAPTER

10
9
8
7
6
5
4
3
2
1

By the end of this chapter, students should have achieved the following objectives:

▶ Describe the different methods of involvement for traditional and online learners.

▶ Discuss the importance of involvement and class participation.

▶ Explain the three types of memory.

▶ Describe some of the methods for improving your memory.

▶ Explain how to improve reading skills.

▶ Explain how to improve writing skills.

▶ Define *plagiarism*, and describe how to avoid it.

▶ Name two editorial styles for properly citing reference resources.

▶ Explain how and where to conduct research online.

▶ Discuss methods for taking tests effectively.

▶ Describe the importance of fieldwork to your online education.

▶ Explain how to maximize success when working in a group.

TOPIC SCENARIO

Image copyright Thomas Peter Voss, 2009. Used under license from shutterstock.com

6

Ed has been retired for almost a year. All of his working life, he looked forward to retirement, and now that he is retired, he misses working. Ed's son got him a computer as a holiday gift, but mostly he just uses it to e-mail his grandkids. Ed struggles with isolation and not feeling useful.

Ed heard that you can "take college classes on the computer" from one of his neighbors but isn't sure what she meant. He has been out of school for a long time and wonders if he has retained all his academic skills. One of Ed's interests has always been foreign languages and culture. He suspects that if he got the proper certifications, he could work part time as a substitute language teacher at any of the local schools. This would increase his interactivity levels and his sense of purpose too.

Based on Ed's situation, answer the following questions:

▶ Where could Ed go to find out more information about online education?

▶ What resources and skills would Ed need to develop and/or brush up on before beginning a certification program?

▶ How could higher education impact nonacademic areas of Ed's life?

We all have time machines. Some take us back; they're called memories. Some take us forward; they're called dreams.

—Jeremy Irons
(Oscar award-winning actor)

SKILLS FOR SUCCESS

Chapters 4 and 5 focused on the importance of your uniqueness. You've probably heard the saying that you can't get by on looks alone. The same is true for personality. It's essential that you know and develop your personality, but there are also some core skills you need to ensure your success.

GETTING INVOLVED

At one time in your life, you probably didn't want to stand out. Many of you will recall the vivid feeling of trying to blend in with your desk as a primary school teacher scanned the room for "volunteers" on whom to call. Involvement in your education at the class participation level is both desirable and important. The more you participate, the greater the rewards.

When you participate, by definition, you become part of a larger entity. So, by participating, you do your part to contribute to something greater than you would have accomplished alone. The "part" or role you play as you participate has a lot to do with who you are. When you participate at your discretion, you do so with comfort and ease. When you are pressed to participate in ways that are uncomfortable, you resist and withdraw.

Over the past 20 years, much has been written about the correlation among involvement, participation, and student success. Alexander Astin, an educational researcher at UCLA, was among the first to gather data on the backgrounds and experiences of college

Image copyright Pepper Frangos, 2009. Used under license from shutterstock.com

students in America. In an article he published in the *Journal of College Student Personnel* entitled "Student Involvement: A developmental theory for Higher Education," Astin concludes that "the greater the student's involvement in college, the greater the learning and development".

STRATEGIES FOR INVOLVEMENT

How does involvement manifest itself? How do you know if you are involved in your academic experience? You are involved when you are actively engaged beyond the required minimum. Opportunities for involvement abound in online learning. You just need to know where to look.

Let's focus on the many ways in which you can become involved in the college experience. Study the table to compare involvement opportunities in a traditional campus-based setting with opportunities for online learners.

6

METHODS OF INVOLVEMENT

Traditional Learner Opportunities	Online Learner Opportunities
• **Orientation.** Attend an on-campus orientation day.	• **Orientation.** Enroll in an "introduction to online learning" course.
• **Conversation.** Get acquainted with fellow students in residence facilities.	• **E-mail.** Get acquainted with classmates through e-mail or text messaging.
• **Campus involvement.** Get involved in campus-based clubs and organizations.	• **Community involvement.** Get involved in community-based activities and programs.
• **International education.** Make friends with students from around the globe.	• **International education.** Work on educational projects with students from around the globe.
• **Career.** Get involved in your career through studies, field experience, and so on.	• **Career.** Get involved in your career through studies, field experience, and so on.

Image copyright digitalskillet, 2009. Used under license from shutterstock.com

6

YOUR ATTENDANCE TENDENCY

When we consider attendance, we generally assume it is about being physically present. But, attending can mean more than just showing up. It is being somewhere and attending to what is going on at the moment.

Have you ever been physically present in class but mentally absent? If your focus tends to drift when a topic loses interest or value for you, think carefully about both your physical presence and mental attending tendencies. When engaged in online learning, you are operating more independently; therefore, it is important that you contemplate how best to keep yourself attending to your academic obligations.

PARTICIPATION STRATEGIES

Now let's examine participation. What are the observable traits that students demonstrate when they participate? Participation is fundamental to the learning process. You must actually become involved in your online coursework and you must make that coursework relevant for you to really learn. Read the comparisons of participation in traditional classroom settings to participation in the online learning environment.

Traditional Methods of Class Participation

1. Sit in a seat in the front of the room, near the teacher so that you can see and hear the teacher well and the teacher sees and hears you.

2. Make regular eye contact with the teacher. Nod your head in affirmation, demonstrating that you are listening and understanding.

3. Raise your hand, pose questions to the teacher, and answer questions posed by the teacher.

4. Become involved in classroom discussions; share your thoughts and observations with your teacher.

5. Be there. Attendance is a prerequisite for participation.

6. Take notes that capture discussion or lecture points of importance.

Online Methods of Class Participation

▶ **Be visible.** Unlike a traditional classroom where simply showing up counts, if you don't contribute in online learning, no one knows you are there. Think through your contributions, and state them effectively. Your presence online is defined by what you say and when you say it.

▶ **Be responsible.** Much of the responsibility for learning is assumed by the teacher in a traditional classroom. Online learning shifts much of that responsibility to you. Learn to pose questions and seek out answers. In online learning, you're a learning facilitator. You assume responsibility for the depth and breadth of your learning.

▶ **Be a contributor.** Passive behavior does not necessarily affect the learning process of all students in a traditional classroom, but it does have a negative impact in online learning. Much of the richest learning takes place among students, sharing the results of their work in the online environment. Enthusiasm is generated through discoveries. *Contribute to the collective body of knowledge by sharing what you learn with your fellow students.*

As an online learner, more of the responsibility for your education is shifted to you. So, if you haven't embraced some of these tried and true strategies, this is a great opportunity to start.

YOUR MEMORY

You will be exposed to a great deal of information in your online program. Your computer becomes your desktop library where you save documents and course materials. Just like a regular library, you have files that you can search. Keeping a solid organized library will be helpful in your online program and beyond.

Yet some content will need to be committed to memory. In all programs, there are key facts and ideas you will need to remember. These facts and ideas will be of regular use to you and will shape your response to the work that you do. That's why they need to be embedded in your thought process for future access.

HOW MEMORY FUNCTIONS

Let's look at our memory and how it operates. Then you can decide how to make your memory serve you best.

▶ **Sensory memory.** Before you can remember something, you must first become aware of it by way of your senses. You have

REFLECTION QUESTIONS

- How do you memorize information? Do you use different methods depending on what you are trying to memorize?
- Do you think the methods you use work best, or would trying some other methods be helpful?

6

6

to see, hear, taste, or smell something and let your brain process what it has encountered. Much of what is perceived in our sensory memory is not stored in our brains.

▶ **Short-term memory.** Short-term memory captures information we are currently using. It holds onto information briefly to help us through the tasks at hand. Most of the information, which enters our short-term memories, is not stored in our brains.

▶ **Long-term memory.** Some material in short-term memory makes it into long-term memory. Information is organized and categorized in our brains in a fashion similar to files on our desktops. These memories make their way from short-term to long-term storage through repetition and association.

Just as there are different ways to absorb information, there are different ways to retain it.

▶ **Repeat it.** To meet up with a classmate whose home you've never been to, you print out a Google map. You use it the first few times you drive there, you glance at it after that, and then you no longer need it. Through repetition, you have committed the information to your memory.

▶ **Make it distinct.** Try to seize upon what makes the information unique. Does the person you are studying have an unusual name? You will recall what stands out.

▶ **Visualize it.** Watch video clips that present the information. Make your own chart of statistics using freeware or graph-building Web sites. Draw flowcharts and timelines.

▶ **Listen to it.** If your lessons are available as streaming audio or a podcast, terrific. If not, why not create your own audio study guide using your computer's microphone input or a handheld recorder. Through conception, recording, and playback, you'll become an expert—and possibly very popular among your peers.

▶ **Write it down.** Scrolling through screens and screens of information might have you seeing stars. First, don't forget to rest your eyes (see Chapter 8). Then, use your computer's word-processing program or notepad software to make an outline of the important points.

success steps

MEMORY STRATEGIES FOR ONLINE LEARNING

1. Use repetition to commit information to your memory.

2. Think about what makes the information unique.

3. Use visual clues and references.

4. Use your auditory memory.

5. Write an outline of the points you need to remember.

 Apply **It!**

Your Memory

Goal: To test out a new strategy for improving your memory.

STEP 1: Pick a form of information that you need to remember. This could be related to your schoolwork, or it could be a grocery list, driving directions, phone numbers, and so on.

STEP 2: Use one of the new strategies for improving your memory to retain the information.

6

READING

REFLECTION QUESTIONS

- What is your attitude toward reading? Do you ever read for pleasure?
- Do you ever fall behind in your assigned reading? In what ways could your reading techniques be improved?

A large part of the knowledge you will acquire in your online program will come from reading. You will read some sources online. Other sources, such as books, will be read offline. You will want to become familiar with the following strategies to discover the ones that work best for you.

▶ **Print it out.** If you find you have difficulty reading onscreen, or you are uncomfortable sitting in front of your computer for long stretches of time, consider printing out your assignment. This gives you many more options for when and how you read. Look for "print-friendly" or "PDF" versions that are meant to look good on paper.

▶ **Scan quickly.** Scan the entire selection to get a quick overview of your assignment. Read titles, subtitles, and anything in bold font. Read the introductory comments and concluding text or summary. You have just gathered a lot of information in a short amount of time!

▶ **Get visual.** Look at pictures, figures, charts, or graphs to get a better grasp on the message. Visual images may be easier for you to remember than words.

▶ **Find a purpose.** Give a purpose to your reading. If you notice a heading that says "Reading Techniques," ask yourself, "What techniques could make *me* successful? Why should I learn this?"

▶ **Quiz yourself.** Take a section that you have read and make up some questions about the reading. Later, ask yourself these questions to see if you remember the answers.

▶ **Make it meaningful.** It is easier to stick to the task of reading when it has meaning for you. As you read the material, search for links between what you have read and how it relates to your own situation.

▶ **Take notes.** Take notes as you read. This process helps you remember important facts. It also gives you an outline to follow when studying for exams. If you are reading online, save your source as an electronic file.

▶ **Say it aloud.** Reciting the most important details of what you have read helps you to remember them. Repeat information aloud to yourself to store it in your long-term memory.

▶ **Share.** Tell someone else about what you have read. The act of explaining makes it more "real" for you and easier to remember.

▶ **Review.** If the reading has a summary, decide if it matches your impression of what you have read. If not, go back and re-read the source to deepen your understanding.

▶ **Reflect.** What you read stays with you much longer and becomes more meaningful if you reflect on what you have just read. Put in your own words what you now know, think, or feel as the result of reading.

success steps

READING STRATEGIES FOR ONLINE LEARNING

1. Read the concepts rather than reading every word.

2. Skim the material first for an overview and to get the general idea.

3. Quiz yourself over the material that you have read.

4. Use various activities to reinforce your learning. Summarize, make diagrams, and apply the information to practical situations.

5. Direct your attention to the areas in which you need the most study and review.

6

WRITING

Writing is a major way in which you indicate what you have learned in your online program. From formal papers to journals to e-mail messages, you will want to express yourself powerfully as you write.

▶ **Create talking points.** Outline your thoughts before you begin. Loosely construct a list of points to be included in the introduction of your paper. Develop a hard-hitting, well-documented conclusion.

▶ **Use writing aids.** Refer to online dictionaries and thesauruses to find just the right words to convey your ideas. Use an online style guide when you have questions about sentence structure or how to list citations.

▶ **Find quality resources.** The Internet is a great place to find resources and reference material, but keep in mind that anyone can post anything. Just because it is online, doesn't mean it is accurate. Research your sources to be sure that they are worthy. Ask yourself: "Who is the author? What is the site's purpose? Is the information up-to-date? Can I tell how old the source is?"

▶ **Wait to review.** After you have finished your writing, it's tempting to give it a quick check and submit it so that you can mark it off your list of things to do. Instead, allow time to pass before you re-read it. This lets you critique your writing with a fresh perspective. Don't be surprised if you find better ways to organize your thoughts.

▶ **Seek critique.** Approach a friend or family member who may be willing to critique your writing. Or, your school may offer this form of assistance through a peer tutor or mentor. Encourage constructive comments about the style and substance of your writing as well as feedback on the mechanics such as typos, grammatical mistakes, and punctuation errors. Be open to these suggestions.

▶ **Express yourself.** You may be asked to keep a journal or Web log (blog) to document your experiences. Blogging gets you in the habit of regularly writing and receiving feedback in the form of comments. (For more on blogging, see Chapter 3.)

REFLECTION QUESTION

• In what ways does writing figure into your life? Consider everything you write, from e-mails to grocery lists to short stories.

▶ **Choose smart software.** Choose software to write your paper that has built-in features such as spell checking and grammar. Spell-checking programs have their limitations and can inadvertently alter the meaning of your sentences by replacing misspelled words with words you do not want. After your electronic spell-check is complete, do it again with your own eyes. If you are asked to follow a particular format, check to see if there is a template available for you to use. The template may aid you in formatting such items as footnotes, references, and headers.

▶ **Don't plagiarize.** Plagiarism is the unauthorized use of someone else's words as if they were your own. It takes only a few seconds to "cut and paste" text from an online source into your electronic paper, but the repercussions—including failure and expulsion—will last years. Review the content you are reading and express the concepts in your own words.

▶ **Submit your work.** Know the teacher's rules for submitting your writing. Do you need to use a particular software application or writing template when generating your paper? Is your paper to be submitted online in a specific way, such as an attachment to an e-mail message? The rules will vary, so be sure that you know what is expected of you.

6

success steps

WRITING STRATEGIES FOR ONLINE LEARNING

1. Outline your thoughts before you begin.

2. Refer to online dictionaries, thesauruses, and style guides.

3. Find quality online sources for your research.

4. Allow time to pass before critiquing your writing.

5. Be open to constructive criticism from others.

6. Get in the habit of regularly expressing yourself through writing.

7. Investigate helpful writing software.

8. Don't plagiarize: Review the content you are reading and express the concepts in your own words.

9. Know the deadlines and the rules for what is expected of you.

PLAGIARISM

Plagiarism is using another person's work as your own without giving appropriate credit to the author or source in a citation or reference. Instructors can easily spot plagiarized work, and all colleges have a strict disciplinary policy against plagiarism. The punishment for plagiarism extends further than school though. Plagiarism is a violation of copyright law. Examples of plagiarism include the following:

▶ Using another author's information and stating that you wrote or created it

▶ Using another author's information and failing to cite it appropriately

▶ Using a direct quotation without quotation marks

▶ Using a diagram, illustration, or photograph without citing it properly

▶ Using material from the Internet without documenting it

▶ Paraphrasing information from a source without stating where the information was obtained

PLAGIARISM VERSUS PARAPHRASING

To paraphrase text is to restate or reword it in another form. Paraphrasing is acceptable when you restate it accurately in your own words and cite the original source. Paraphrasing is plagiarism when you only change a few words, reorder the text, and/or fail to cite the source of the original passage.

If you are quoting a source directly, do not paraphrase. Instead, cite the source in your text, and put the quotation in quotation marks. Failing to punctuate the quote with quotation marks can be construed as plagiarism.

Most students don't plagiarize intentionally. To avoid making mistakes when citing sources, take good notes upfront. The Online Writing Lab at Purdue University recommends marking up your research notes with a legend that corresponds to the sources. For instance:

▶ Q for a quotation

▶ S1 for source 1

▶ ME for personal insights

GIVING CREDIT WHERE CREDIT IS DUE

In almost all cases, if you did not come up with the idea yourself, you need to give credit to the person or entity that did. The following chart illustrates this point.

Need to Cite	Do Not Need to Cite
• When you use someone else's words or ideas, whether published or unpublished	• When you write about your own experiences, thoughts, and conclusions in your own words
• When you reprint diagrams, charts, and pictures	• When you create, draw, or photograph your own visuals and diagrams
• When you use a direct quotation or exact phrase specific to someone else	• When you use common knowledge or material that exists in the public domain

As you may note, there are a couple of situations where you don't need to cite the source of original content: common knowledge and public domain.

Common Knowledge

Common facts that can be found in numerous places and are likely to be known by a lot of people do not require a citation. However, if the information is not generally known, a direct quotation about something that is general knowledge, or an interpretive statement about general knowledge, you do need to cite the source.

Public Domain

Public domain refers to work in which no one maintains proprietary interests or legal ownership over a work. A creative work is said to be in the public domain if no laws restrict its use by the public. The public domain comprises writing, art, music, inventions, and more. Sometimes media ends up in the public domain when its copyright expires, or if the work or its subject matter is specifically excluded from existing laws. You can find tons of free books, movies, and music online by searching in the public domain.

Free to Use, Not to Abuse

Common knowledge and information from the public domain are free to use but not to abuse. It's also a misnomer that anything on the Internet is public domain, and text can be lifted from all Web sites as "fair use." If you use information from the Internet, you must credit the source. Remember, failing to cite the source is plagiarism, may break the law, and is also a disservice to you and your classmates. We learn best through the development of our own ideas, not by blindly copying and pasting passages of text.

success steps

STRATEGIES FOR AVOIDING PLAGIARISM

1. Know what constitutes plagiarism.

2. Paraphrase in your own words, and check your paraphrase against the source text.

3. Put direct quotations in quotation marks.

4. Cite your sources appropriately.

Apply **It!**

Plagiarism Research

Goal: To develop a better understanding of what plagiarism is and how to avoid it.

STEP 1: Using the Internet, research more about what constitutes plagiarism and how you can avoid it as a student.

STEP 2: Research related current topics such as "open-source," "creative commons license," and "public domain use."

STEP 3: Write a blog entry, or start a discussion with a friend about these topics.

ATTRIBUTION

When writing research papers, any information taken from an outside source—quotations, facts, and ideas that aren't common knowledge—must be attributed to its source.

6

There are many acceptable styles of attribution—enough to fill entire books on the subject. Most English and humanities classes use the Modern Language Associate (MLA) style, whereas social science classes often uses the American Psychological Association (APA) style. The MLA recommends a concise in-text citation, typically featuring the page number. The APA recommends an author/date style of in-text citation.

The rules for citing source materials are very specific, but luckily you're not required to memorize them. Whether you're citing a book with three authors or a Web article with no author, there are guidelines for how to do it. For some basics, see the MLA and APA appendices at the end of this book. For a thorough guide to citation styles, see Diana Hacker's *A Writer's Reference* (6th ed.), or visit the following Web sites:

▶ http://apastyle.apa.org/
▶ http://www.mla.org/style

INTERNET RESEARCH

The Internet has made researching easier by providing access to a wide variety of information from the comfort of your own home. This is especially beneficial to online learners who may not have access to a traditional campus library.

INTERNET SEARCH ENGINES

Understanding how to search for information is essential to effective researching. The library has a card catalog; the Internet has a search engine. A search engine is an information retrieval system. They provide an interface where users can specify criteria about an item of interest and have the engine find and return matching items. In the most popular form of search, items are documents or Web pages, and the criteria are words or concepts that the documents may contain.

There are search engines for Web sites, blogs, people, news, shopping, real estate, and legal and medical documents. Google and Yahoo! are two of the most popular search engines, but there are almost as many search engines as the virtual content they provide for use. For a current list of search engines, usefully categorized by type and style, visit Wikipedia.com, and look at the current "List of Search Engines."

Electronic Searching Techniques

There are some basic techniques that can help focus or expand a search using a search engine. To define your search terms more precisely, use Boolean operators such as AND, OR, and NOT. The operator AND is used to retrieve results where *all* the words separated by AND are included. The operator OR is used to retrieve results where either of the words separated by OR are included. Finally, the operator NOT is used to retrieve results where the word preceded by NOT is excluded. Implied Boolean operators include using a plus sign (+) in front of a word to retrieve results that include the words and a minus sign (−) in front of a word to retrieve results that exclude the word, similar to the AND and NOT operators. Quotation marks around phrases are used to retrieve results where that specific phrase is included. Most search tools have an "Advanced Search" link that provides a form to help focus or narrow the searches. These advanced search tips and tools explain the search language used by that particular search tool.

success steps

STEPS FOR EXPLORING THE USE OF BOOLEAN OPERATORS

1. Select a topic you would like to research. The topic should be identified by a phrase. "MyPyramid" is an example.

2. Experiment with the various Boolean operators, both in words and symbols. For example, use "food guide + pyramid"; then try "food guide not pyramid" and compare your results.

3. Try other searches specific to your field. Experiment with various combinations of search terms and operators to gain an understanding of the types of results you obtain.

4. Note your observations regarding the results you obtain using different operators in your searches. Note which results would be most useful in various situations.

Source: From 100% *Student Success* 1st edition by SOLOMON/TYLER/TAYLOR/QUANTUM INTEGRATIONS. 2007. Reprinted with permission of Delmar Learning, a division of Thomson Learning: www.thomsonrights.com. Fax 800 730-2215.

RESOURCES AVAILABLE ON THE INTERNET

Many of the resources available in traditional libraries are now available on the Internet through virtual libraries, subject directories, and Web sites. There are numerous free sites and fee-based sites that provide information-literate users with valuable resources at their fingertips. This easy, convenient access is especially helpful to online learners who may conduct research at hours when traditional libraries are closed.

Online Reference Resources

Reference resources such as dictionaries, thesauruses, encyclopedias, almanacs, maps, handbooks, and directories can all be accessed online. A countless number of general and subject-specific resources are available, covering every industry. A few popular resources include the following:

- http://www.dictionary.com
- http://www.thesaurus.com
- http://www.encyclopedia.com
- http://www.en.wikipedia.org
- http://www.almanac.com
- http://www.infoplease.com
- http://www.factmonster.com

Online Periodicals

Many magazines and newspapers now maintain a presence online, often with extra features such as additional content, photo out-takes, and movies. Try searching for your favorite entertainment or sports magazine online to see what you can find.

Some of the individual online magazines and periodical search engines require a subscription. Many other sites have full-text articles (http://www.onlinenewspapers.com) available free. The Internet Public Library (http://www.ipl.org) maintains a mission to provide library services to Internet users. In addition to traditional reference resources, such as dictionaries and encyclopedias, they host a collection of magazines from art and humanities to science and technology.

Professional and Trade Organizations

Professional and trade organizations are groups whose members share similar interests or occupations. These organizations are excellent research resources for students because they feature updated information, trends, practices, and networking opportunities for a given industry. Virtually all organizations have some kind of online presence. In fact, these days, the validity and relevance of an organization may be measured by the presence and quality of its Web site. Students can keep current in their field by participating in a professional organization's activities and learning about issues at the forefront of the industry.

To find professional and trade organizations online, try searching based on your interests, for instance, "event planner organization" and "construction trade magazine."

---

success steps

STEPS FOR STARTING THE RESEARCH PROCESS

1. Clearly identify the task. If researching a specific project, read the instructions carefully or ask enough questions to understand exactly what the project requires. What is your task? How long does your project need to be? What kind of resources should you use? Are there a specific number of resources required? For what audiences are you writing?

2. Develop the topic in detail. A good start to developing a topic is to frame the task in the form of a question. Next, brainstorm a list of additional questions that could be asked to answer the main question. In the brainstorming phase, do not evaluate or judge the questions, just list them. Then, review the question list and develop the topic more fully. If necessary, read about the topic in the encyclopedia or another broadly focused resource to make sure the background has been reviewed sufficiently.

3. Create an outline of major topics and subtopics. This strategy works well even for minor research tasks. In some cases, the initial questions and outline may change as you find more information.

4. Generate a list of keywords and phrases and subject headings. Organize keywords appropriately to produce a useful list. Refine your search phrases to broaden or narrow the focus as needed. Add to this list as the search continues.

5. Conduct the search using online search engines.

6. Locate the resource online. Review the bibliography of the resources you find to continue finding additional items. Continue revising your search term list and outline as needed.

Source: From 100% *Student Success* 1st edition by SOLOMON/TYLER/TAYLOR/QUANTUM INTEGRATIONS. 2007. Reprinted with permission of Delmar Learning, a division of Thomson Learning: www.thomsonrights.com. Fax 800 730-2215.

EVALUATING ONLINE INFORMATION

Once information is found, it must be evaluated to determine if it is appropriate, credible, and current. Anyone can put information on the Internet. No individual or organization edits, controls, or verifies all the information on the Internet; therefore, it's up to users to evaluate the information they find. At a minimum, researchers should ask the following questions about the Web site from which they get the information, in order to determine the value of the information they find:

- **Sponsorship.** Who or what organization sponsors the Web site and what are their motives for doing so?

- **Authorship.** Who authored the content, and are they qualified to do so?

▶ **Currency.** Is the information dated, revised regularly, and current? Are the original and revision dates on the site? Are the cited resources current?

▶ **Quality of information.** Does the information appear to be high quality? Does it agree with other sources of information you have read?

▶ **Objectivity.** Is the site biased toward a specific viewpoint? Does the site present a viewpoint as fact? Are all viewpoints addressed or just one perspective?

Source: From *100% Student Success* 1st edition by SOLOMON/TYLER/ TAYLOR/QUANTUM INTEGRATIONS. 2007. Reprinted with permission of Delmar Learning, a division of Thomson Learning: www. thomsonrights.com. Fax 800 730-2215.

TEST TAKING

Teachers give tests as a method of evaluating what you have learned. Taking tests may mean you will use your computer to take a test online, or you may be able to download the test, take it, and submit it for grading. Online tests may differ from in-class testing in important ways, so you will need to follow directions carefully.

▶ **Don't cram.** As an online learner, you are responsible for determining when and where you will study. Break your assignments into smaller chunks, and mark on a calendar when you will commit to doing them. Pace your studying over several days or weeks, and then review the material the night before the test.

▶ **Test your technology.** It is critical that you have a reliable connection when taking a test online. If you have problems with your Internet service at home, consider an alternative location where you may take the exam, such as your workplace or library. Be sure you know how to obtain technical support if needed during the test.

▶ **Practice ahead of time.** A computerized test may ask you to enter your responses in ways that are unfamiliar to you. See if there is a practice area where you can answer a sample question before beginning the test.

▶ **Get comfortable.** Become familiar with your technology. For example, not all keyboards have the keys in exactly the same location. Use a keyboard where you feel confident typing your answers. Sit in a chair that is at the correct height and has a comfortable seat. Make sure your screen has no glare. Avoid distractions.

▶ **Know the rules.** Read all of the rules before beginning the test. For example, you may not be able to "browse" through the questions before answering them. Instead, you may be shown only one question at a time, and you must answer it before proceeding. You may not be able to go back and change your answers. There may be a time limit.

▶ **Stay calm.** Anxiety may decrease your concentration and cause you to make mistakes. Get a good night's sleep, eat a nourishing meal, keep to your routine, and tell yourself that you are going to do well. If you have the option to choose when you may take your test, pick a time when you feel you are physically, mentally, and emotionally ready.

▶ **Hunt for feedback.** Some online tests may provide automatic scores and results after you submit them. At other times, you may need to access a special area of the course to see your score. Find out the answers to questions that stumped you so that you are prepared for the final exam.

6

success steps

TEST-TAKING STRATEGIES FOR ONLINE LEARNING

1. Know the amount of time you have to complete the test. Divide the total amount of time that you have by the number of questions on the test to get a general idea of approximately how much time you can spend on each question.

2. Read through the entire test. This will provide you with an overview and general picture of what the test entails. It will also help you effectively allocate your time to each of the questions.

3. Read directions carefully. Misunderstanding test directions can cause you to lose points by using the wrong approach to the questions.

continued

4. Answer the questions that you know first. Doing so gets them "out of the way" so that you can spend more time on items that require more concentration and time. Answering the questions you know may offer insight into more difficult questions.

5. Answer all questions. Even if you are unsure of the entire answer, use the information you do know to provide an answer. Doing so will increase your chances for partial credit.

Apply **It!**

Study Techniques

Goal: To apply study techniques to your learning experience.

STEP 1: Make an honest assessment of your study and test-taking skills. Pinpoint specific areas in which you want to develop your skills.

STEP 2: Using the Internet, research methods for making changes in the areas you identified.

STEP 3: Set specific goals, and create a plan for applying what you learn to your assignments and class work.

STEP 4: Assess your progress, and adjust your goals as needed to continue your improvement.

Image copyright Mathieu Viennet, 2009. Used under license from shutterstock.com

▶ REFLECTION QUESTIONS

- Do you think you have ever suffered from test anxiety? If so, when? Why do you think you were anxious? What did you do to try and relieve your anxiety?
- How good are you at taking exams? How might you be able to improve?

FIELDWORK

Laboratory or fieldwork helps you gain expertise by applying what you have learned in an actual setting. Your teacher may expect you to set up your own experience. For example, it may be up to you to find your own location and make arrangements for a mentor. The location and mentor will need to meet your instructor's criteria for the fieldwork to be accepted.

▶ **Secure locations.** Research and contact organizations and businesses in your community that offer a good match to the experience you are seeking. Explain details such as the nature and proposed duration of your involvement.

▶ **Find mentors.** Mentors understand the industry, and they have a great deal to teach you. Your teacher may provide criteria that the mentor must meet. Make sure you tell your mentor what you want to get out of the experience.

▶ **Don't hide, seek.** Familiarize yourself with the objectives, and make sure that you find ways to achieve them. Let your instructor and mentor know what you are looking to learn in the field, and ask for their assistance in locating quality experiences.

▶ **Stay in touch.** Keep your instructors informed of your progress.

▶ **Do your homework.** Complete and turn in assignments related to your fieldwork as scheduled.

▶ **Report problems.** Report problems as soon as they develop so that your instructors can help you resolve them quickly. It is up to you to initiate communication.

▶ **Keep a journal.** List the competencies you gained formally or informally through the field experience. Your teacher may ask you to document the number of hours you spent doing fieldwork. A journal helps you keep track of these.

▶ **Ask for references.** Your fieldwork shows that it has provided you with some of the knowledge and skills you need for a job. Ask your mentor or fieldwork supervisor for a reference that you can give to potential employers.

6

▶ **Explore employment.** If you want to pursue employment at the fieldwork location, let them know. Inquire about future job opportunities, and leave your contact information.

▶ **Express thanks.** Send thank you e-mails or cards to your mentors or trainers for helping you gain valuable experience. Include any events or individuals who made the experience especially beneficial. You want to leave them with a good impression.

success steps

FIELDWORK STRATEGIES FOR ONLINE LEARNING

1. Secure locations by researching and contacting organizations and businesses in your community.

2. Find mentors who can instruct you.

3. Take initiative and seek out quality experiences.

4. Keep your instructors informed of your progress.

5. Complete and turn in assignments related to your fieldwork as scheduled.

6. Keep a journal detailing your fieldwork experiences.

7. Ask for references, explore employment opportunities, and express thanks.

Image copyright dasilva, 2009. Used under license from shutterstock.com

LECTURES

You may be asked to attend a lecture but not in person. Online presentations are given with videos or slide shows that can be enhanced with audio or text. You choose the time when it's convenient to view them. Some lectures may be presented "live" through video conferencing or other technical means. Frequently, a method is set up for you to ask questions or offer comments.

▶ **View on-demand.** Set aside a time that is convenient for you to watch prerecorded lectures.

▶ **Pace yourself.** Prerecorded lectures can be paused and stopped to take notes or breaks. Go at your own pace.

▶ **Download.** If your online access is slow, find out if you can download lectures for viewing offline after the download is complete. Schedule the download for times when you aren't using the computer, such as when you are at work or asleep.

▶ **Seek adequate access.** If your Internet connection is slow or you have an older computer, it may be hard to get good video picture quality or speed. See if you can watch the lectures on another computer, or check to see if the lectures can be sent to you on a CD-ROM or DVD.

▶ **Grasp the big picture.** First scan prerecorded videos or prepared slides to get a better idea of the theme for a prerecorded lecture, and then watch it again but with more focus on the details.

▶ **Prep your tech.** If you are participating in a real-time conference, be sure that your setup is working properly. Make sure you know how to obtain technical support if something goes wrong.

▶ **Speak up.** Actively participating in a real-time conference helps you stay alert. Make comments where appropriate, keeping in mind that the quality and quantity of your contributions may influence your grade.

▶ **Minimize distractions.** When listening to a lecture, don't check your personal e-mail or pay your bills online. Avoid distraction by taking notes or generating questions for the teacher. Stay focused.

▶ **Follow-up.** After the lecture is over, consider ways in which you can follow up to ensure that you have grasped the meaning. Make sure that you have finished all related assignments.

▶ **Smile for the camera.** If you are attending a videoconference and you are on camera, remember that others are able to see you although you may not be able to see them. Conduct yourself as you would in a classroom.

---

success steps

LECTURE STRATEGIES FOR ONLINE LEARNING

1. View on-demand prerecorded lectures.

2. Go at your own pace.

3. Download lectures for viewing offline after the download is complete.

4. Seek adequate Internet access or CD/DVD alternatives.

5. Grasp the big picture.

6. Prep your tech.

7. Speak up and actively participate.

8. Minimize distractions.

9. Follow up to ensure that you have grasped the meaning.

10. Conduct yourself in a teleconference as you would in a classroom.

PROJECTS AND GROUP WORK

REFLECTION QUESTIONS

• How comfortable are you doing group projects?
• Do you find that you naturally fall into a role (i.e., group leader, recorder, etc.)?

You may be asked to work on a project that involves more than one type of learning activity and that will need to be completed over time. Your teacher may assign the project to a group, which means you must collaborate with peers to finish it successfully. You may need to discover ways to work with your group at a distance.

▶ **Search for success.** Projects often require more research than for other types of activities. Become comfortable using search engines to locate material online.

▶ **Don't ignore offline.** Learn what services are available to you and how to use them. Don't forget about your local library.

▶ **Identify quality.** Learn how to tell a quality resource from a questionable one.

▶ **Get organized.** Projects are complex and involve multitasking. Prepare a flowchart or map that shows how the various aspects of the project relate to each other.

▶ **Set milestones.** Identify tasks to accomplish, and determine when you expect to finish them. Write your milestones on a timeline, and indicate when they have been reached.

▶ **Join forces.** If you are working in a group, arrange with the members when, where, and how you will interact. Agree on methods for communicating and sharing the workload.

▶ **Be the leader.** Being the project leader can give you an experience working with people beyond what you learn from the project itself. Take the time and effort to know your group members, guide them toward tasks that build on their strengths, and assist your peers with things that may challenge them.

▶ **Know your role.** When working in a group, know your responsibilities and accomplish the tasks that go along with it.

▶ **See the big picture.** Although you may be working in a group where you are focused on one aspect or task, stay informed of how the overall project will come together. Find out what other group members are doing, and understand how their activities relate to yours.

▶ **Explore new skills.** Projects provide excellent incentives to gain new experiences. Embrace these opportunities to expand your skills.

6

success steps

PROJECTS AND GROUP WORK STRATEGIES FOR ONLINE LEARNING

1. Decide on a group or team goal.

2. Use individual talents and experiences in a collaborative effort to achieve a balanced blend of talent to meet the group goal.

continued

3. Balance the individual and team needs, and communicate clearly about both.

4. Address and resolve conflict as soon as possible.

5. Involve all participants in decisions.

6. Emphasize commitment to the successful achievement of the team goal.

CHAPTER SUMMARY

This chapter provided information to help you improve your practical learning skills and habits. Strategies for developing your memory, reading, writing, researching, and test-taking skills were also introduced. This chapter emphasized the importance of working with others—both in fieldwork assignments and group projects—and using online tools to enhance your learning. By honing your ability to work as part of a team and mastering Internet technology now, you are setting yourself up for future success in your career.

6

POINTS TO KEEP IN MIND

In this chapter, several main points were discussed in detail:

- ❯ Students who excel academically have typically developed skills in efficiently taking notes, completing reading and writing assignments, studying, taking exams, and working well in groups.

- ❯ Opportunities for involvement abound in online learning. You are involved when you are actively engaged beyond the required minimum. When you participate, by definition, you become part of a larger entity.

- ❯ Information is learned more effectively when it is organized, both in your computer and in your mind.

- ❯ Plagiarism can have extreme consequences. When completing writing assignments, make sure to describe your thoughts in your own words and properly cite your resources.

- ❯ The Internet is a vast trove of helpful information. However, it is up to you to evaluate and verify the quality, accuracy, and relevancy of the information you find.

- ❯ Teamwork is a requirement of both academic and professional environments. Start by being a team player now.

- ❯ Fieldwork can be an enriching component of your online education but often requires initiative on your part.

6

LEARNING OBJECTIVES REVISITED

Review the learning objectives for this chapter, and rate your level of achievement for each objective using the rating scale provided. For each objective on which you do not rate yourself as a 3, outline a plan of action that you will take to fully achieve the objective. Include a time frame for this plan.

1 = did not successfully achieve objective

2 = understand what is needed, but need more study or practice

3 = achieved learning objective thoroughly

	1	2	3
Describe the different methods of involvement for traditional and online learners.	☐	☐	☐
Discuss the importance of involvement and class participation.	☐	☐	☐
Explain the three types of memory.	☐	☐	☐
Describe some of the methods for improving your memory.	☐	☐	☐
Explain how to improve reading skills.	☐	☐	☐
Explain how to improve writing skills.	☐	☐	☐
Define *plagiarism*.	☐	☐	☐
Name two editorial styles for properly citing reference resources.	☐	☐	☐
Explain how and where to conduct research online.	☐	☐	☐
Discuss methods for taking tests effectively.	☐	☐	☐
Describe the importance of fieldwork to your online education.	☐	☐	☐
Explain how to maximize success when working in a group.	☐	☐	☐

Steps to Achieve Unmet Objectives

Steps   Due Date

1. _____   _____

2. _____   _____

3. _____   _____

4. _____   _____

5. _____   _____

6. _____   _____

7. _____   _____

REFERENCES

Astin, A. Student involvement: A developmental theory for higher education. *Journal of College Student Personnel,* 157, 297–308.

Conley, D. T. (2003). Understanding university success. Standards for Success, A project of the Association of American Universities and The Pew Charitable Trusts.

Downing, S. (2005). *On course strategies for creating success in college and in life* (4th ed.). Houghton Mifflin Company.

Guilbert, S. D. (2001). *How to be a successful online student.* McGraw-Hill.

Hacker, D. (2006). *A Writer's Reference* (6th ed.). Boston: Bedford Books of St. Martin's Press

Kelly, K. (2006, May 14). Scan this book! *New York Times.*

Leshin, C. B. (1998). *Student resource guide to the Internet, student success online.* Prentice Hall.

Purdue University Online Writing Lab. Avoiding Plagiarism. Retrieved April 1, 2004, from http://owl.english.purdue.edu/handouts/research/r_plagiar.html

Raimes, A. (1996). *Keys for writers: A brief handbook.* Boston: Houghton Mifflin.

Tracy, B. (2004). *Time power: A proven system for getting more done in less time than you ever thought possible.* Amacon.

Wahlstrom, Williams, & Shea. (2003). *The successful distance learning student.* Wadsworth/Thomson Learning.

White & Baker. (2004). *The student guide to successful online learning.* Pearson Education, Inc.

6

CHAPTER OUTLINE

7 Common Concerns of the Online Learner

LEARNING OBJECTIVES

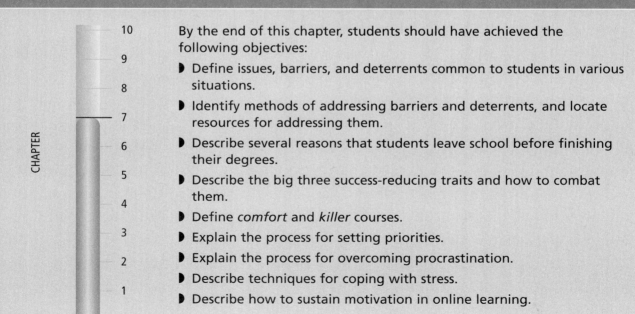

By the end of this chapter, students should have achieved the following objectives:

▶ Define issues, barriers, and deterrents common to students in various situations.

▶ Identify methods of addressing barriers and deterrents, and locate resources for addressing them.

▶ Describe several reasons that students leave school before finishing their degrees.

▶ Describe the big three success-reducing traits and how to combat them.

▶ Define *comfort* and *killer* courses.

▶ Explain the process for setting priorities.

▶ Explain the process for overcoming procrastination.

▶ Describe techniques for coping with stress.

▶ Describe how to sustain motivation in online learning.

TOPIC SCENARIO

Laura is a single mother who works as a receptionist at a doctor's office. She recently enrolled in the nursing program at an online college. Laura's daughter is in daycare while Laura works. One night a week, she exchanges babysitting with another mother in her neighborhood. Laura tries to cram all of her studying into this night and is having trouble keeping up. She hasn't gotten a good night's sleep in months, and her grades are starting to slip. She has had to work overtime at the doctor's office to afford the college tuition. Before she can even get to the interesting nursing classes, she has to take all the "foundation" classes, and she is struggling with these. When Laura considers all these factors, she starts to feel negative and wonders if she will be able to finish the program.

Based on Laura's situation, answer the following questions:

▶ Think about your own personal situation. How do Laura's challenges relate to those that you face?

▶ How can Laura find a way to balance all of her responsibilities? What are some resources that might be available to her?

▶ How can negative thinking have an adverse affect on Laura's success?

Image copyright Ami Beyer, 2009. Used under license from shutterstock.com

7

If you're trying to achieve, there will be roadblocks. I've had them; everybody has had them. But obstacles don't have to stop you. If you run into a wall, don't turn around and give up. Figure out how to climb it, go through it, or work around it.

—Michael Jordan
(considered by many to be the greatest American basketball player of all time)

BARRIERS AND DETERRENTS TO ONLINE LEARNING

To fully understand academic success, we must consider the obstacles. Many factors contribute to students staying in school and realizing their goals. Similarly, some factors contribute to students' decisions to leave school. If you've ever failed at anything, you've probably heard the common saying: "If at first you don't succeed, try again." NBA star Michael Jordan put it into more specific terms: "I have missed more than 9,000 shots in my career. I have lost almost 300 games. On 26 occasions, I have been entrusted to take the game winning shot ... and missed. And I have failed over and over and over again in my life. And that is why ... I succeed."

STAYING THE COURSE

Vincent Tinto, a Distinguished University Professor at Syracuse University, is one of the nation's premier authorities on student success. From his post at Syracuse University, Tinto isolated nine factors that contribute to students' decision to leave college. He calls these "forms of departure" and theorizes that they are the major causes of students leaving U.S. colleges today.

FORMS OF DEPARTURE

Tinto's Nine Forms of Departure can be described as follows:

1. **Academic difficulty.** Of all students who leave college across the nation, 20–30% do so because they are unable to adjust to the academic landscape. They are not yet ready

Image copyright Yuri Arcurs, 2009. Used under license from shutterstock.com

7

to succeed in academia and need further skill development. The remaining 70–80% of leavers are described in one or more of the following categories.

2. **Adjustment.** Some students who leave early are unable to make a successful transition to college. They may feel under prepared for the demands of college life. Problems here may be transitory or chronic. These students need help in making the transition to more independent functioning, such as decision making and problem management.

3. **Goals.** Not all students enter college with well-defined goals and a belief in the importance of goal completion. Some students have goals that are not in line with the goals the institution expects them to have. Another group of students will change their goals while in college. Therefore, unformulated goals, short-term goals, or changed goals may lead to early departure from college.

4. **Uncertainty.** Many college students begin their study with vague reasons for having done so. Lack of purpose undermines some students' willingness to persist to goal completion.

5. **Commitments.** Completion of a college degree requires effort. Not all students are willing to expend the time and energy necessary to complete their degree requirements.

6. **Finances.** Lack of financial resources to commit to college places pressure on many college students today. Many students conclude that the cost of attending college outweighs the benefit.

7. **Integration and community membership.** Lack of integration into the schools' population can undermine commitment and speed students' departure from college.

8. **Incongruence.** Incongruence results when the individual student finds that his interactions do not support his needs. This arises when the institution is seen as too challenging or, conversely, not challenging enough.

9. **Isolation.** Isolation occurs when the student and other members of the institution do not connect. Many students express feeling apart from the mainstream. Lack of contact with caring faculty contributes to a student's experience of isolation.

▶ REFLECTION QUESTION

- Which of Tinto's Nine Forms of Departure do you think could apply to you? How might you go about turning them around?

STAYING IN SCHOOL

Failure is by no means the end of the line. In fact, it's actually just another method of self-analysis. Let's apply some positivism from Chapter 1 to Tinto's Nine Forms of Departure.

1. **Academic readiness.** Many online learners bring real world and job skills to the academic experience. Foundation classes are usually available to brush up on core subjects and writing skills. Also, by reading this book, you are showing initiative and developing many of the qualities that will ready you for your college experience!

2. **Preparedness.** One of the many advantages to online learning is the ability to go at your own pace. Many students at traditional colleges can find themselves unable to keep up. Online learning offers you flexibility, and many schools provide administrative support and trouble-shooting.

3. **Goals.** By enrolling in online college, you are likely looking to make developments in your personal and professional life. This, in itself, is a goal. By using the techniques in this book, you have learned to assess your long-term goals and monitor your progress on short-term goals.

4. **Certainty.** Whereas some students at traditional colleges enroll because they think they're supposed to or someone else wanted them to, your decision to go to online college is one that you made. You may have been responding to the advice of a colleague, friend, or mentor, but ultimately you have made a decision to move forward in your goals and pursue your degree.

5. **Commitments.** Completion of a college degree requires effort. Luckily, online education gives you flexibility to work at your own pace and on your own time. You can structure your program in a way that fits your lifestyle. With these advantages, you are more likely to honor your commitments.

6. **Financial aid and incentives.** Chapter 9 discusses the costs and benefits of getting a college degree. The career benefits alone can include better pay, more skills, job advancement, and job security. Many financial aid resources are available for online education, including scholarships and grants.

7

7. **Integration and community membership.** Online education has unique and modern ways of fostering community. Whereas face-to-face social situations can sometimes feel daunting and awkward; e-mail, bulletin boards, and social networks are great ways to create and grow relationships with your classmates and peers. Chapter 2 offers more information on community development.

8. **Congruence.** Combat incongruence by selecting a mixture of "comfort" and "killer" classes. Reward yourself for tough required courses with electives that stimulate your interests.

9. **Connecting with others.** Online education gives you the unique opportunity to connect with an assortment of people who transcend age, class, and geographic categorizations. Take advantage of this by getting to know people who bring a different background to your shared (or even unshared) interests. Today's workforce is increasingly diverse. Connecting with others well and often now will prepare you for a career in the future.

Apply **It!**

Monitoring Perceptions and Responses

Goal: To increase your awareness of your responses to deterrents and maximize productive responses.

STEP 1: Create a three-column table in a word-processing document on your computer. In the left-hand column, write a list of the deterrents that you personally face. In the middle column, identify and describe how you react to that deterrent. For example, if you are struggling with finances (the deterrent), and you react by being late with rent and feeling frustrated, describe that in the middle column. In the right-hand column, record alternative reactions and solutions to that deterrent, for example, researching your financial aid options.

STEP 2: Reflect on the deterrents, responses, and alternatives that you have listed. Make it a point to be conscious and aware of the list you have made.

STEP 3: When you face one of your deterrents, recall your list. If you are a visual person, consider carrying the list with you as a reference. Take a few seconds to monitor your response and consider whether it is the most productive response you can make. Consider the alternative responses and actions that you recorded.

STEP 4: Replace any nonproductive emotional response with your constructive alternative response. Note your emotional response when you take the more productive action.

STEP 5: Record your progress in the document in another table. Over time, you should see a change in your initial responses to deterrents that you encounter.

THE BIG THREE SUCCESS-REDUCING TRAITS

Tinto told us nine reasons why students leave college. However, many students stay the course but fall prey to patterns of stagnation. John Light, a nationally known educator and futurist, identified three traits that most often impede learning and success in higher education: negative thinking, diminishing productivity, and complacency. You must eliminate these success-reducing traits to attain your goals. They prevent success in college, on the job, and in life. Let's review how they operate and how best to turn them around.

NEGATIVE THINKING

Negative thinking occurs when you think the worst will happen. When you see the dark side of a situation, you immobilize yourself with worry, doubt, and fatalism. Some online students have learned to think negatively. They focus on problems rather than seeing opportunities. Negative thinking undermines the success of online students because it reduces self-confidence. When you hear someone say, "I can't," or "It won't work," those are everyday examples of negative thinking. If you believe your own negative self-talk, you limit your horizons.

Negative thinking causes you to:

▶ Establish a failure scenario.

▶ Predict that it will come true.

▶ Take limited action or no action to alter the outcomes from failure to success.

▶ Find that you are correct and that failure occurs.

If you are starting to feel overwhelmed, take a few steps back from the situation. Are there other avenues you can explore to get around the problem? Can you seek out the advice of an instructor or mentor? Try to be as mindful of your attitude as you would in your workplace or among members of your community whom you respect. When you establish a success scenario, you encourage yourself to take action and bring your dreams to fruition.

▶ REFLECTION QUESTION

• Think of a time when you felt very negative about your prospects in a situation. How did that situation turn out for you? What steps could you have taken to achieve a better result?

success steps

NIP NEGATIVE THINKING IN THE BUD!

1. Maintain a positive attitude.

2. Keep your long-term goal (and its payoffs) in mind.

3. Brainstorm creative solutions to your problems.

4. Reward yourself for short-term successes and positive thinking.

DIMINISHING PRODUCTIVITY

Some online students experience a drop in productivity as they progress throughout their program. They begin with enthusiasm as they start their new journey, but enthusiasm wanes when the newness wears off. These online students are on a path of diminishing productivity. They are placing less time and less energy into their online coursework. The diminished output is evident to faculty and peer groups alike. The pattern creates conditions where poor performance and likelihood for attrition can occur.

If you are starting to feel apathetic, don't give up. It's natural to experience ebbs and flows in enthusiasm throughout life. You might not notice this is happening until a tangible indication—like

Image copyright Terence, 2009. Used under license from shutterstock.com

a drop in grades—occurs. Try to approach your studies with an alert and invested attitude at all times. When you feel a change, consider factors that could be influencing it. Are you not feeling challenged enough? Are your resources spread thin from taking on too much of a challenge? Are external circumstances (health, job, family, finances) involved?

Sometimes putting yourself in a productive mode encourages you to keep it up. You may need to kick start your productivity if it stalls.

REFLECTION QUESTIONS

- What areas of your life and health could contribute to diminishing academic productivity?
- How can you be proactive about maintaining good productivity levels?

7

success steps

STAYING PRODUCTIVE

1. Review your goals to ensure that you are on track.

2. Know your priorities and understand how to determine when some are more pressing than others.

3. Assess your overall situation, including your studies, health, job, family, finances, and other factors.

4. Make thoughtful decisions regarding prioritizing, and communicate professionally about your needs.

continued

5. Understand the natural ebb and flow of enthusiasm. If you didn't experience the occasional indifference, you wouldn't know how passion felt either.

6. Revisit the setup for the last time you felt productive, and put yourself back in that mode.

COMPLACENCY

Some online students set modest performance goals for themselves. They aim low, fail to stretch, and set the stage for falling below standard. The complacent online student does only the minimum amount of work required. This type of attitude disappoints peer groups and faculty members alike. Because it is impossible to precisely calculate the least amount of work to do to pass, students who do this can often end up failing.

Chances are, you didn't enroll in online college to be complacent. You did it to develop yourself toward a more enriching future. So set the bar high. Michael Jordan has said, "You have to expect things of yourself before you can do them." Imagine one of the biggest jumps or most impressive dunks you have seen or heard attributed to Jordan. Now imagine him casually and carelessly tossing a basketball into a basket that only came up to his neck in height. Translate that image into your own life. You want to aim for what is possible, not easy. You will only ever achieve a fleeting sense of gratification for goals that lack challenge.

success steps

AIM HIGH

1. Set goals based on things that are important to you and that you desire.

2. Set your goals high enough to be challenging, but make them reasonable enough to be achievable.

3. State your goals positively, and share them with people in your life.

4. Write down your goals. Written goals serve as a reminder, a motivator, and an indicator of your progress.

Image copyright Factoria singular fotografia, 2009. Used under license from shutterstock.com

MANAGING RESOURCES

What you do with your time and where you direct your energy dictates much of your future; yet most people never think about it. Even worse, some people come to the conclusion that they don't have enough time or energy to get things done at all. One of the most important lessons to be learned in life is that we all have the same amount of time. What differs in each of us is how we choose to use it.

The way we view and handle time has a lot to do with our personalities. Some people choose to move throughout time fluidly, whereas others find it helpful to structure their time. You probably know people who need reminders to do things and others who do not. It is important to recognize that we are all different in our responses to techniques for handling time. In short, what works for one person may not work at all for another.

 Apply **It!**

Resource Brainstorming

Goal: Create a resource bank for common student needs.

STEP 1: Start a group of peers who share the desire to create a resource bank for common student needs. These can

continued

Image copyright BelleMedia, 2009. Used under license from shutterstock.com

include things like notes for missed classes, financial aid tips, and daycare.

STEP 2: Decide on a format for the group. You may want to create an e-mail listserv or start your own MySpace group. The format should work for all group members, and all group members should be able to get access and contribute.

STEP 3: Share ideas and information regarding resources that group members might find helpful. Members can post needs in a classified ad style or post useful information in an archives section.

STRATEGIES FOR TIME MANAGEMENT

It is common for people to keep track of their money in ledgers and spreadsheets, but tracking time is a less widespread practice. When people make impulsive or thoughtless purchases, they have products, receipts, or bank statements to show for it. Because time is intangible, spending time thoughtlessly gives way to the excuse, "time simply got away from me." In truth, you have more control of time than you think.

TIME ANALYSIS

The first step to time management is analysis. Time analysis can be as basic as jotting down a table of how you spend blocks of time during the week or using a daily planner or online calendar to reflect on your activities. The important thing is to note wasted or misused time, as well as unexpected openings in your schedule.

After you know how you actually spend your time, you can redesign your schedule. Start by assessing the amount of time each task requires. Next, schedule tasks with the appropriate amount of time reserved. If your calendar gets crowded, you will need to determine which tasks are more essential than others. This process is known as prioritizing.

SETTING PRIORITIES

Most instructors know that students juggle a variety of commitments, and they recognize that life sometimes makes demands other than those related to school. The students' responsibility is to prioritize coursework along with other life responsibilities. Problems arise when students make excuses, and when other aspects of life continually take priority over school assignments.

Instructors have to comply with certain regulations, and this limits how flexible they can be with students. Students who consistently neglect school responsibilities put instructors in a precarious situation. This can result in policies that are restrictive and seem disrespectful of students' other commitments. It is important to set your priorities responsibly and to communicate your reasons and intentions to your instructor.

7

success steps

SETTING PRIORITIES

1. Know your priorities, and understand how to determine when some are more pressing than others.
2. Make thoughtful decisions regarding prioritizing, and communicate professionally with instructors about your needs.
3. Understand the deterrents that online learners commonly face during their education.

continued

REFLECTION QUESTIONS

- How well do you balance your priorities?
- What questions do you ask yourself to prioritize your responsibilities?
- How do you resolve conflicting priorities?

4. Understand your responses to deterrents, and select a constructive response from your resources.

5. Develop professional behaviors and a professional presentation style.

OVERCOMING PROCRASTINATION

Procrastination is a slippery slope. Putting something off until tomorrow that you could or should do today results in more tasks being pushed back, more missed deadlines, and a tremendous decline in productivity. It's understandable to be less than enthused about unenjoyable activities. However, starting them in a timely manner gives you more control, more time, and less stress. By completing your least favorite tasks first, you can move on to the reward of more enjoyable activities.

success steps

OVERCOMING PROCRASTINATION

1. Prioritize your tasks by making a realistic daily schedule or to-do list.

2. Set deadlines. It's a good idea to set both starting and finishing deadlines. As some tasks may not be completed in a day, your finishing deadline will give you an idea, over time, if you are staying on track.

3. Dive right in. Get the least enjoyable task—the one you're most likely to procrastinate—out of the way. Consider breaking it up into smaller steps to get you started. If cleaning the house is the task, begin with the dishes in the sink, and then move on.

4. Reward yourself for your accomplishments.

DISTRACTIONS AND DEMANDS

These days, distractions are everywhere—from your always-on Internet connection to the handheld devices you carry in your pocket.

Ironically, what was meant to increase your productivity often results in significant distraction. When you sit down at your computer to start a project, the lure of e-mail, eBay, youtube, games, or CNN can be quite compelling.

Managing your time wisely means knowing when to work and when to play. Although there's no harm in taking breaks to read your favorite blog, you must take care not to let distraction overwhelm action. Action means sticking to your priorities and to-do lists. Reward yourself for a job well-done by bidding on that auction item or watching a funny video *after* you accomplish the task. Search online for freeware that filters or blocks distracting Web sites during your study time.

It's not just the Web that's distracting, it's the world itself. The people in your life are entitled to your attention, and part of time management involves dealing with the demands of others. If you know you have a family obligation, allocate for this time as you would for a school project. If a friend calls while you are studying, ask if you can get back to him or her later. There are times when you simply will not be able to accommodate the demands of others, and that's okay. Learning to be assertive and managing distractions and demands will help you accomplish your goals in school and in life.

PLANNING AND ENERGIZING YOUR TIME ONLINE

The disconnect between setting high priorities and under-allocating time derails us on our path to success. Your highest priorities need to take up most of your time. You need to be honest with yourself about your style of time management and adopt a process that will work for you. If that isn't happening, then something needs to change.

Do you remember Gittinger's emotional procedural dimension from Chapter 5? It identifies our tendencies to be role-regulated and structured with time or more role-flexible and fluid with time allocations. Gittinger provides insight into how time management is an individualized issue that is linked to personality.

Read the following table carefully to understand the thinking and activity patterns of basic level personality difference on the procedural dimension. Locate the descriptors that fit you best, and think about how these preferences affect your time, not style.

	Uncompensated Regulated	Compensated Flexible	Uncompensated Flexible	Compensated Regulated
View of World	Sees world in a matter of fact way.	Sees reality in terms of absolutes.	Sees world relativistically.	Sees world moralistically.
Patterns of Thinking	Logic—tight, clear thinker.	Works to be unemotional and objective in decision making.	Flexible, conceptual thinker sees the forest more than the trees.	Complicated thinker. Diagrams and maps complex solutions.
Patterns of Activity	Naturally depends on procedure, protocol.	Develops own procedure.	Admires procedure if purposeful.	Demands flexibility, interested in procedures for their sake.
Task Follow-Through	Follows through if personally interested or if required to do so.	Compulsively follows through; resists being directed but likes to direct others.	Needs strict deadlines to follow up. Rarely feels that tasks are satisfactorily completed.	Initially distractible. Meets deadlines. Adheres to procedure and pleases authority.

FINDING YOUR PEAK PRODUCTIVITY PERIOD

We all need energy to succeed. But what is energy, and where does it come from? There are really two forms of energy. First, there is mental energy—the kind that comes from cultivating your intellectual resources. Second is physical energy—the kind that comes from being healthy, rested, and strong. To perform at peak productivity, you need both forms of energy.

You have learned about how time and energy management is important to success. Now let's explore how time and energy management practices can work best for you. You have a time of day when you are most productive. That is your peak productivity time. Too often, we attempt to squeeze our online academic time around everything else in our lives. The result is that we are attempting our most complex cognitive work at times when we are least able to perform.

How many times have you attended to family, friends, or work responsibilities and left your least preferred time for online learning? If your education matters to you, it deserves to be scheduled at times when you are fresh and can get the most from the experience!

What makes this complex is that peak productivity times vary with the individual. Some people are morning people. They think better and more clearly immediately after a good night's sleep. For

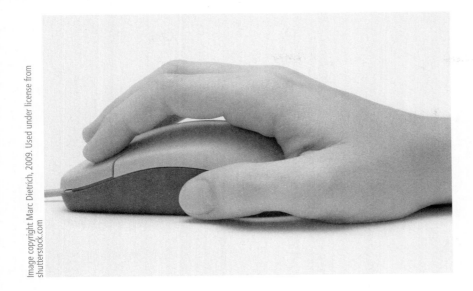

Image copyright Marc Dietrich, 2009. Used under license from shutterstock.com

others late morning or mid-day is the time when their minds start clicking. And then, there are the night owls who come out late and do their best work while others are winding down.

IDENTIFYING COMFORT AND KILLER COURSES

Not all courses are created equal. Some online classes do not require as much time and energy as others. Mix the two for a recipe for success.

Comfort Courses

"Comfort" courses are often the ones you look forward to the most. They are the courses in which you do not expect to struggle. Comfort courses pertain to the field of study you have chosen. They may sometimes include electives that indulge an interest outside of your major, such as music or film appreciation.

Killer Courses

The courses that you look forward to least can be described as "killer" courses. They are the ones that resonate least with you as a student. They are courses in which you expect to struggle. Killer courses may be requirements for your major. You must take them to complete your program but would not choose them otherwise.

▶ REFLECTION QUESTION

• Are you a "morning person"? Are you a "night owl"? Do you feel energized or sluggish after a meal?

▶ REFLECTION QUESTION

• Why do you think that a course that may be difficult for one person may be easy for another?

COPING WITH STRESS

Time management, knowing your peak productivity periods, and choosing a mixture of comfort and killer courses are all ways to cut down on stress. Stress, however, is a part of life. Stress is physical, mental, or emotional strain or tension that occurs when a person has trouble coping with a situation, event, or change. In an increasingly busy world, stressors bombard us all. Your goal is not to eliminate all stress entirely but to find better ways to cope with a normal amount.

CAUSES OF STRESS

Uncertain, unpredictable, and uncontrollable events are often stressful. Some specific conditions that can lead to stress include the following:

- Health problems
- Relationship problems
- Job changes
- Life changes

It's vital to acknowledge that stress is a problem and treat it. When stress is secondary to a condition like those in the preceding list, you put yourself in a weakened state to deal with the primary issue. Research has shown that stress is a contributing factor in heart disease, ulcers, poor memory, and diminished immune function. Healing from physical or emotional troubles is much harder when stress is involved.

STRESS RELIEF

Learning to cope with stress benefits you in all aspects of life. Stress relief is not just good for reducing tension; it is also an important part of your healthy lifestyle. For more information on achieving optimum health, see Chapter 8.

Addressing the Cause

Certain stressors can be eliminated. Rush hour commuting is undoubtedly a source of stress for many people. It may be possible to avoid the gridlock by joining a carpool, driving in off-peak hours, or working from home.

Simultaneous changes such as moving, increased schoolwork, and new job responsibilities can lead to stress. If too many concurrent events are contributing to stress, see what can be postponed, decreased, or delegated.

Rethinking the Situation

Sometimes it's not possible to remove a stressor from your life. We all have certain obligations, some of which may make us anxious or uncomfortable. In these cases, you need to refocus your energy. If you're worried about flying, use that energy instead to plan activities for your destination. Give yourself a pep talk, and take a break from the stressful situation.

Relaxation Techniques

There is a lot you can do to reduce your stress with little money or instruction. Try one or more of the following to see what works for you:

▶ Meditation

▶ Deep breathing

7

▶ Yoga

▶ Journaling

▶ Aerobic activity

SUSTAINING MOTIVATION IN ONLINE LEARNING

You have heard it said that if you love your work, you'll never work a day in your life. This means that you find your work interesting. Fortunately, we do not all find the same things to be of interest. Some of us are interested in research or investigative work, and some are drawn to artistic expression and creative pursuits. Some embrace the world of business and finance, and some prefer practical, realistic endeavors. Still others want to help people to better their lives. Our uniquely defined set of interests is related to our personality dynamics and the environmental exposure we have received.

When you find something to be of interest, you engage in it freely and often. You are willing to commit your time in pursuit of your interests. Think about the television shows you watch, the books you read, the Web sites you visit, and how you spend your leisure time. You spend your time in activities that hold your interest. So, examining your current interests is an important part of being successful. That's because you are likely to invest time where you have interests. And how you spend your time is one of the factors that determine success.

success steps

MAINTAINING MOTIVATION

1. Clearly identify your motivators.

2. Ensure that your motivators are realistic. For example, if you identify a reward for yourself, make sure it is something you can realistically do or afford.

3. Keep your motivators "top of the mind" so that they remain visible and you are aware of them.

CHAPTER SUMMARY

This chapter addressed deterrents that often pose difficulties for students who are getting an education while fulfilling numerous other life responsibilities. Ways to maintain productivity, positivism, and motivation were discussed. Managing your resources, energy, and time in accordance with your personality type were suggested. As you move on from this text, keep your alternative responses to deterrents in mind. Over time, your reactions to deterrents will change on your path to success.

POINTS TO KEEP IN MIND

In this chapter, several main points were discussed in detail:

▶ Online learners must balance a variety of life priorities such as school, family, and career.

▶ Although all priorities are important, some priorities become more pressing at times. Communicate openly about your needs with your instructors.

7

▶ Time management, knowing your peak productivity periods, and choosing a mixture of comfort and killer courses are all ways to cut down on stress.

▶ Nip negative thinking in the bud by maintaining a positive attitude and sustained motivation.

▶ Consider your personality type when planning your time, energy, and resource management.

▶ Assess the deterrents that you face, and use appropriate resources to address them.

LEARNING OBJECTIVES REVISITED

Review the learning objectives for this chapter, and rate your level of achievement for each objective using the rating scale provided. For each objective on which you do not rate yourself as a 3, outline a plan of action that you will take to fully achieve the objective. Include a time frame for this plan.

1 = did not successfully achieve objective

2 = understand what is needed, but need more study or practice

3 = achieved learning objective thoroughly

	1	2	3
Define issues, barriers, and deterrents common to students in various situations.	☐	☐	☐
Identify methods of addressing barriers and deterrents, and locate resources for addressing them.	☐	☐	☐
Describe several reasons that students leave school before finishing their degrees.	☐	☐	☐
Describe the big three success-reducing traits and how to combat them.	☐	☐	☐
Define *comfort* and *killer* courses.	☐	☐	☐
Explain the process for setting priorities.	☐	☐	☐
Describe how to sustain motivation in online learning.	☐	☐	☐
Explain the process for overcoming procrastination.	☐	☐	☐
Describe techniques for coping with stress.	☐	☐	☐

Steps to Achieve Unmet Objectives

Steps   Due Date

1. _____   _____
2. _____   _____
3. _____   _____
4. _____   _____
5. _____   _____
6. _____   _____
7. _____   _____

REFERENCES

Adler, J. (1999, June 14). Stress. *Newsweek,* pp. 56–63.

Astin, A. W. (1993). *What matters in college?* Jossey-Bass.

Bryson & Havens. (2005). Relieving Stress. Retrieved from WebMd: http://www.webmd.com/balance/Stress-Management/ Stress-Management-Relieving-Stress

Redenbach, S. Self-esteem and emotional intelligence: The necessary ingredients for success. Esteem Seminars Programs.

Stone & Hill. (1960). Success through a positive mental attitude. Retrieved from http://en.wikiquote.org/wiki/Success_Through_ a_Positive_Mental_Attitude

Throop & Castellucci. (2004). *Reaching your potential: Personal and professional development.* (3rd ed.). Thomson Delmar Learning.

Tinto, V. Educational communities and student success in the first year of university. Retrieved from Syracuse University: http:// www.monash.edu.au/transition/activities/tinto.html

Tracy, B. (2004). *Time power: A proven system for getting more done in less time than you ever thought possible.* Amacon.

7

CHAPTER OUTLINE

Nutrition, Fitness, and Wellness: An Overview

Nutrition: You Are What (When and Where) You Eat

Exercise: Commit to Being Fit

Wellness: Mind, Body, and Spirit Health

Health Considerations for the Online Student

8

CHAPTER

THE BIG PICTURE

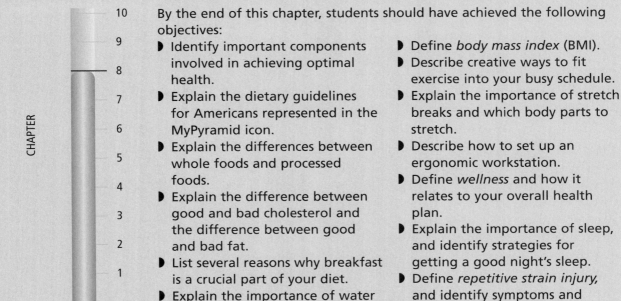

LEARNING OBJECTIVES

By the end of this chapter, students should have achieved the following objectives:

- Identify important components involved in achieving optimal health.
- Explain the dietary guidelines for Americans represented in the MyPyramid icon.
- Explain the differences between whole foods and processed foods.
- Explain the difference between good and bad cholesterol and the difference between good and bad fat.
- List several reasons why breakfast is a crucial part of your diet.
- Explain the importance of water in your nutrition plan.

- Define *body mass index* (BMI).
- Describe creative ways to fit exercise into your busy schedule.
- Explain the importance of stretch breaks and which body parts to stretch.
- Describe how to set up an ergonomic workstation.
- Define *wellness* and how it relates to your overall health plan.
- Explain the importance of sleep, and identify strategies for getting a good night's sleep.
- Define *repetitive strain injury*, and identify symptoms and methods of prevention.

TOPIC SCENARIO

Gabe always knew he carried a few extra pounds, but recently his doctor measured his body mass index and told him he was overweight. The doctor did lab work and informed Gabe that he had high bad cholesterol and low good cholesterol. Based on these risk factors for disease, the doctor recommended he exercise more and lose some weight. Between work, being a single dad, and his night classes online, Gabe doesn't have much time to exercise or prepare healthy meals. He usually has lunch at a fast food chain near work. He eats a frozen dinner at the computer while studying late at night. The most exercise he gets is walking down the driveway to his car.

Based on Gabe's situation, answer the following questions:

▶ What did Gabe's doctor mean by "body mass index"?

▶ What did Gabe's doctor mean by "good and bad cholesterol"?

▶ What are some things about Gabe's lifestyle that contribute to him being overweight?

▶ What changes could Gabe make in his diet?

▶ What changes could Gabe make in his lifestyle to include more exercise?

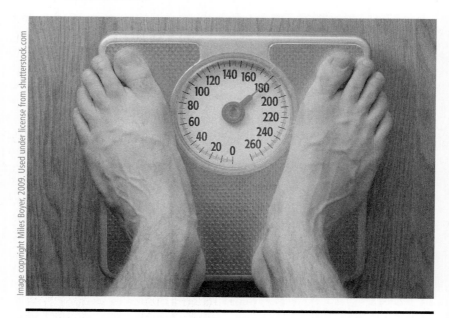

Image copyright Miles Boyer, 2009. Used under license from shutterstock.com

8

Eating everything you want is not that much fun. When you live a life with no boundaries, there's less joy. If you can eat anything you want to, what's the fun in eating anything you want to?

—Tom Hanks,
actor (Esquire, 2006)

NUTRITION, FITNESS, AND WELLNESS: AN OVERVIEW

You've heard it said, "If you don't have your health, you don't have anything." That's because your health is the foundation on which everything else about you is built. As a college student, stress, lack of sleep, an unhealthy diet, and a sedentary lifestyle can quickly turn that foundation from sturdy sheetrock into flimsy paperboard. Positive health habits reinforce your foundation and contribute directly to your academic success.

NUTRITION: YOU ARE WHAT (WHEN AND WHERE) YOU EAT

We develop patterns of behavior, such as eating habits, over time. Some of us, for instance, may regularly skip breakfast or grab something at a drive-thru. Skipping meals, budget limitations, and easy access to fast food and large portions contribute to erratic and unhealthy eating patterns. At times, we don't eat a healthy diet because we don't know what food is good for us. This chapter will touch briefly on the major points. With the Internet skills you've developed as an online learner, in-depth information is always just a keystroke away.

DIETARY GUIDELINES

The U.S. Department of Agriculture (USDA) in conjunction with the U.S. Department of Health and Human Services regularly publishes a set of dietary guidelines designed to reduce and prevent death and disease in Americans. A healthy serving of nutritional information can be found in the USDA's food pyramid at http://www.mypyramid.gov/index.html.

Image copyright Denis Pepin, 2009. Used under license from shutterstock.com

MyPyramid.gov
STEPS TO A HEALTHIER YOU

The current version of the food pyramid, MyPyramid, acts as a reminder to make healthy food choices and be active every day. The icon emphasizes moderation, proportionality, and variety—keys to a healthy diet. MyPyramid uses your age, gender, height, and weight to create a customized recommendation of grains, vegetables, fruit, milk, meat, and beans for a balanced diet.

Apply **It!**

Three-Day Diet and Exercise Record

Goal: To analyze your diet and exercise to help in determining areas where you are doing great and areas where improvements could be made.

STEP 1: Schedule three consecutive days for your diet and exercise record. Be sure that two of the days reflect normal work/school days and that the third day reflects a weekend day or a day off. Try to choose days that will represent your typical diet and exercise behaviors.

STEP 2: Keep a small journal with you throughout the day and take notes on time, food and portion size, and exercise activity level and duration. Include every food and beverage you consume, as well as all types of physical activity, including walking, gardening, and housework.

8

STEP 3: Open an account at a Web site such as http://www. fitday.com, where you can track your diet, exercise, weight loss, and goals in a free online diet journal. Rather than having to look up calorie counts yourself, this free service provides detailed nutrition information on thousands of foods, long-term diet analysis, and easy-to-read charts and graphs of your progress.

STEP 4: Answer the following questions:

a. Where did the bulk of your calories come from?

b. Are you meeting the requirements suggested by the MyPyramid guide?

c. Were you surprised by the data on calories and/or portion size for any of your favorite foods?

d. Were you surprised by how some of the activities you do each day can contribute to calories burned?

STEP 5: Consider keeping the journal going to meet your goals for good nutrition, peak fitness, and/or weight loss. You can even make your "diary" public and let your friends see your progress.

WHAT, WHEN, AND WHERE YOU EAT

We all know the adage, "You are what you eat." Next time you reach for that bag of chips, take a look at the ingredients. How many of them do you recognize? If you are what you eat, do you know what you are?

What You Eat

The USDA recommends that half of the grains (bread, rice, cereal) you eat each day be whole grains. Whole grains differ from refined grains in that they contain dietary fiber (for intestinal health), iron (for strength), and B-vitamins (for immunity). Refined grains have been processed and stripped of these qualities to give them a longer shelf life.

Processing accounts for the artificial flavors and colors and unpronounceable chemicals that show up on the ingredients list of many common foods we eat. By contrast, whole foods have not been processed: they have nothing added and nothing taken away. Whole foods can prevent disease, provide our cells with energy, and build our immunity.

> **REFLECTION QUESTIONS**
>
> • Open your kitchen cabinets and take out a few items. Review the list of ingredients. Do you know what everything is? Review the suggested serving size. How does it compare to your idea of portion size?
>
> • Open your refrigerator. Review the expiration dates. Is there a connection between a food that is perishable (has a short shelf life) and ingredients you recognize?

Image copyright Branislav Senic, 2009. Used under license from shutterstock.com

8

Short On Time?

▶ Prepare meals in advance and store them in containers in the fridge. Try following quick recipes at http://www.studentrecipes.com and http://www.yumyum.com.

▶ Why wait on checkout lines when you can select your groceries online and have them delivered? Many national chains from Albertsons to Safeway offer delivery service. Try an online search for "grocery delivery" and your city. FreshDirect (New York), Plumgood Foods (Nashville), and Organic Express (San Francisco area) all offer healthy and organic grocery delivery services.

▶ Not much of a cook? Franchises are springing up across the map to help you out. You can show up at one of these "kitchens," and cook a month's worth of meals with their recipes, ingredients, utensils, and takeout containers. If you're truly kitchen-shy, you can save time *and* money by getting a month's worth of family-sized entrees as takeout: http://www.supersuppers.com and http://www.dinnersready.com.

Vitamins?

Vitamins can be a good supplement for people with specific diets, such as vegetarians. However, vitamins are not a substitute for a healthy and balanced meal plan. Food gives our bodies a spectrum of easily absorbed nutrients, vitamins, and minerals. In certain situations,

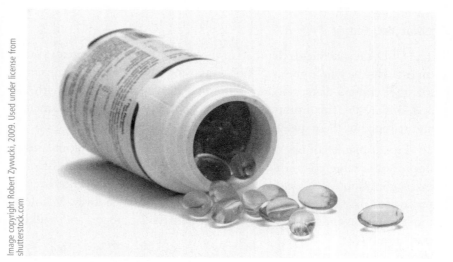

Image copyright Robert Zywucki, 2009. Used under license from shutterstock.com

8

vitamins and supplements may be beneficial. For instance, Vitamin C can lessen the duration of a cold, B12 may fight off the detriments of stress, and calcium can guard against osteoporosis. That said, a multi-vitamin won't cancel out that milkshake you just had.

Fat and Cholesterol: The Good and the Bad

Beware of fat-free foods. When fat is taken out, something else is put back in—and that's usually sugar. A proclamation of "fat-free" on the front of the package is a marketing fact, so check the back of the package for nutrition facts. Often fat-free foods are processed to the point of containing completely unrecognizable ingredients. Some fat in your diet is good; saturated and trans fats, however, are not. Trans fats are a side effect of partially hydrogenated oils and are found in foods such as peanut butter. This type of fat is considered more of a health risk than naturally occurring fats and can put you at risk for heart disease.

Like fat, cholesterol also comes in good and bad versions. Cholesterol is actually a healthy part of your body and contributes to cell and hormone formation. However, if too much LDL (bad) cholesterol circulates in your blood stream, it can clog your arteries and lead to a heart attack or stroke. Conversely, HDL (good) cholesterol moves away from the arteries, through the liver, and out of your body. A high level of HDL

REFLECTION QUESTION

- Think about the foods you eat. Are you eating a varied and nutrient-rich diet? Are there any particular nutrients or vitamins your diet lacks? Can you think of a food source that would provide that nutrient or vitamin? (For instance, oranges provide Vitamin C, milk provides calcium, and spinach is rich in iron.)

8

▶ REFLECTION QUESTIONS

- Do you eat breakfast? Why or why not?
- How many meals do you eat each day? Do you find yourself hungry or snacking in between?

8

▶ REFLECTION QUESTIONS

- Where do you eat your meals?
- Are you a fast or slow eater?

cholesterol may protect against heart attacks. The online student who lives on a fast food/low exercise lifestyle is especially at risk for an undesirable cholesterol count. You can lower your LDL cholesterol by limiting your intake of foods from animals (eggs, meat, poultry, etc.) and raise your HDL cholesterol by engaging in regular physical activity.

When You Eat

You've heard that breakfast is the most important meal of the day. Studies show that students who eat breakfast do better in school and are more likely to maintain a healthy weight. Eating a good breakfast of protein and fiber fuels your body and keeps you feeling full until lunchtime. If you skip breakfast, you may find yourself snacking on high-sugar fixes that provide temporary energy and a big crash.

Eating several small meals throughout the day is a great way to keep your body nourished and your energy sustained. Nuts, yogurt, cheese sticks, and apples make good between-meal snacks.

You'll also want to avoid eating too late at night. Late-night calories are not expended and lead to weight gain. Heavy or spicy meals before bed can cause sleep disturbances.

Where You Eat

Eating while using the computer may have become a habit. You may think you are fueling your body by munching on high calorie snacks or drinking caffeinated beverages while studying, but ultimately these can contribute to problems such as lack of concentration. Break this cycle by making a rule that you will not eat or drink while at the keyboard. This rule will also encourage you to get up, move around, and perhaps engage in some exercise when you do decide to eat and drink. As a bonus, you will not have to worry about crumbs in your keyboard or spilling coffee on your laptop.

PROPER HYDRATION

Your body is made up of about 60% water. Drinking eight glasses of water a day is necessary for good health. Water aids in digestion, eases back and joint pain, maintains muscle tone, supports clear skin, supplies oxygen and nutrients to your cells, and rids your body of waste.

Because water contains no calories, can serve as an appetite suppressant, and helps the body metabolize stored fat, it directly contributes

Image copyright Sklep Spozywczy, 2009. Used under license from shutterstock.com

to weight loss. If that's not reason enough to love H_2O, consider that dehydration slows down your metabolism and results in fatigue, short-term memory loss, and trouble focusing.

Having trouble switching from soda to water? Try these tips:

▶ Use a straw to drink more without feeling like it.

▶ Add a slice of lemon or lime to give water some taste.

▶ Try drinking at room temperature: it goes down easier.

If, despite all the obvious health benefits, zero calories, and zero cost, you still struggle with drinking eight glasses of water, consider purchasing a gadget like the HydraCoach (http://www.hydracoach.com), which "calculates your personal hydration needs, tracks your real-time fluid consumption, paces you throughout the day, and motivates you to achieve and maintain optimal hydration."

REFLECTION QUESTIONS

- How many beverages do you drink each day?
- How much of that is water?

8

success steps

NUTRITION GUIDELINES FOR THE ONLINE LEARNER

1. Use the MyPyramid example to guide your food choices.

2. Eat a varied and nutrient-rich diet with an emphasis on whole foods.

continued

3. Consider preparing meals in advance so that you can eat them when you're short on time.

4. Get a routine physical checkup where your doctor can test your cholesterol and check for any other nutrient deficiencies that might require vitamin supplementation.

5. Don't skip breakfast.

6. Eat several small meals throughout the day to maintain your energy.

7. Drink plenty of water (at least eight glasses per day).

EXERCISE: COMMIT TO BEING FIT

Most Americans are overweight because of their sedentary lifestyles. While our ancestors burned calories by walking and performing outdoor labor, we ride in cars and sit. As an online learner, you need to recognize when to move away from the keyboard. Your body needs physical exercise to continue to function at optimal levels. When you are physically fit, you have the required energy to carry out daily tasks without tiring. You also have the energy to enjoy what you are doing.

COMMIT TO BE FIT

Body Mass Index (BMI) is one of the most accurate ways to determine when extra pounds translate into health risks. BMI is a measurement using a person's weight and height to gauge total body fat in adults. Someone with a BMI of 26 to 27 is about 20% overweight, which carries moderate health risks. A BMI of 30 and higher is considered obese. With a high BMI, you are at an increased risk of developing additional health problems. Calculate your BMI here: http://www.nhlbisupport.com/bmi/.

Putting the "Fit" in "Fitness"

In addition to your studies, you may be balancing one or more jobs, a family, social commitments, and other responsibilities. When, you ask, are you expected to fit in fitness?

▶ REFLECTION QUESTIONS

- How much time do you currently spend exercising? Is this an area in which you could improve?
- Are there any aspects of your daily routine you could change to include more exercise (i.e., biking to work, walking to the grocery store)?

8

Body Mass Index Table

	Normal						Overweight					Obese										Extreme Obesity															
BMI	19	20	21	22	23	24	25	26	27	28	29	30	31	32	33	34	35	36	37	38	39	40	41	42	43	44	45	46	47	48	49	50	51	52	53	54
Height (inches)													Body Weight (pounds)																							
58	91	96	100	105	110	115	119	124	129	134	138	143	148	153	158	162	167	172	177	181	186	191	196	201	205	210	215	220	224	229	234	239	244	248	253	258
59	94	99	104	109	114	119	124	128	133	138	143	148	153	158	163	168	173	178	183	188	193	198	203	208	212	217	222	227	232	237	242	247	252	257	262	267
60	97	102	107	112	118	123	128	133	138	143	148	153	158	163	168	174	179	184	189	194	199	204	209	215	220	225	230	235	240	245	250	255	261	266	271	276
61	100	106	111	116	122	127	132	137	143	148	153	158	164	169	174	180	185	190	195	201	206	211	217	222	227	232	238	243	248	254	259	264	269	275	280	285
62	104	109	115	120	126	131	136	142	147	153	158	164	169	175	180	186	191	196	202	207	213	218	224	229	235	240	246	251	256	262	267	273	278	284	289	295
63	107	113	118	124	130	135	141	146	152	158	163	169	175	180	186	191	197	203	208	214	220	225	231	237	242	248	254	259	265	270	278	282	287	293	299	304
64	110	116	122	128	134	140	145	151	157	163	169	174	180	186	192	197	204	209	215	221	227	232	238	244	250	256	262	267	273	279	285	291	296	302	308	314
65	114	120	126	132	138	144	150	156	162	168	174	180	186	192	198	204	210	216	222	228	234	240	246	252	258	264	270	276	282	288	294	300	306	312	318	324
66	118	124	130	136	142	148	155	161	167	173	179	186	192	198	204	210	216	223	229	235	241	247	253	260	266	272	278	284	291	297	303	309	315	322	328	334
67	121	127	134	140	146	153	159	166	172	178	185	191	198	204	211	217	223	230	236	242	249	255	261	268	274	280	287	293	299	306	312	319	325	331	338	344
68	125	131	138	144	151	158	164	171	177	184	190	197	203	210	216	223	230	236	243	249	256	262	269	276	282	289	295	302	308	315	322	328	335	341	348	354
69	128	135	142	149	155	162	169	176	182	189	196	203	209	216	223	230	236	243	250	257	263	270	277	284	291	297	304	311	318	324	331	338	345	351	358	365
70	132	139	146	153	160	167	174	181	188	195	202	209	216	222	229	236	243	250	257	264	271	278	285	292	299	306	313	320	327	334	341	348	355	362	369	376
71	136	143	150	157	165	172	179	186	193	200	208	215	222	229	236	243	250	257	265	272	279	286	293	301	308	315	322	329	338	343	351	358	365	372	379	386
72	140	147	154	162	169	177	184	191	199	206	213	221	228	235	242	250	258	265	272	279	287	294	302	309	316	324	331	338	346	353	361	368	375	383	390	397
73	144	151	159	166	174	182	189	197	204	212	219	227	235	242	250	257	265	272	280	288	295	302	310	318	325	333	340	348	355	363	371	378	386	393	401	408
74	148	155	163	171	179	186	194	202	210	218	225	233	241	249	256	264	272	280	287	295	303	311	319	326	334	342	350	358	365	373	381	389	396	404	412	420
75	152	160	168	176	184	192	200	208	216	224	232	240	248	256	264	272	279	287	295	303	311	319	327	335	343	351	359	367	375	383	391	399	407	415	423	431
76	156	164	172	180	189	197	205	213	221	230	238	246	254	263	271	279	287	295	304	312	320	328	336	344	353	361	369	377	385	394	402	410	418	426	435	443

Source: Adapted from *Clinical Guidelines on the Identification, Evaluation, and Treatment of Overweight and Obesity in Adults: The Evidence Report.*

Chapter 7 offers advice on time management, but when it comes to fitness, the advice is to be creative. Perhaps you are familiar with some of the following household activities:

- Mowing the lawn
- Gardening or pruning
- Scrubbing floors or washing windows
- Dusting or vacuuming

All of the above, which you likely already do, burn calories. Add a few activities from the following list and you'll be fitting in fitness before you know it:

- Walk to the bank or post office rather than driving.
- Ride your bike to the grocery store.
- Invite a friend to go for a weekly jog.

8

> Join a sports league for adults, or start a regular sports night with your family.

Learn While You Burn

As an online learner, you have no reason to gain the "freshman 15"—the weight the average traditional college freshman puts on. Instead of dormitories and lecture halls, you've chosen the freedom of an online education—the world is your classroom.

In place of coffee and a donut, try heading to the gym in the morning. Most of the cardio machines have a ledge for your textbooks or laptop. No gym membership? No problem. If you have a desktop computer, a treadmill, and a wireless mouse, scroll while you stroll. Morning exercise is as invigorating as it is beneficial: not only will you kick start your day, but you'll burn the most calories.

It's a fact that some students are morning people, and others are night people. One is not better than the other; rather it's best that you recognize when you're at peak performance. Your online education affords you the flexibility to learn on your schedule. Some gyms are open 24 hours. Take advantage of the slow hours when you'll have the least crowds and the most access to equipment.

Check with your instructors to see if any lessons are available as podcasts. Podcasts are audio/video presentations that can be streamed on your iPod or mp3 player. Listen to your lessons while going for a hike or bike ride.

Most importantly, find ways to engage in physical activity, and make them part of your routine.

STRETCH BREAKS

There are occasions when you may have to be at your computer for several hours at a time. As a general rule, you should get up and stretch every half hour. There are free programs you can download to remind you of your stretch breaks. You should alternate stretching the following body parts:

> Neck and face
> Wrists and hands
> Shoulders and arms

Image copyright Adrian Moisei, 2009. Used under license from shutterstock.com

▶ Legs and ankles

▶ Back

Besides tension relief and defense against injury, stretching elongates muscles, preparing them for growth. Keep a few freeweights or a resistance band by your workstation for a quick upper body workout on your stretch break.

Don't forget about stretching your eyes! Step away from the screen for 15 minutes during each 2-hour period or for 10 minutes per hour of intensive work. Remember to blink your eyes periodically to avoid dry eyes and eyestrain.

 Apply **It!**

Stretch Out

Goal: To take a break from your studies and stretch.

STEP 1: Connect to the Internet, and search for "stretching exercises." A good site to visit is http://www.ergocise.com. Just click Stretch Now to view a list of suggested stretches with illustrations.

continued

STEP 2: If you have any preexisting conditions (i.e., bad back, jaw disorder), consult your physician before beginning a stretch program.

STEP 3: Try spending a few minutes stretching your neck, eyes, wrists, and so on. If any particular body part feels particularly sore, pay special attention to it and use a low-impact stretch to relieve tension.

STEP 4: Using an automated program or a schedule of your own design, develop a habit of frequent stretch breaks.

success steps

CREATIVE FITNESS FOR THE ONLINE LEARNER

1. Find ways to "fit in fitness."
2. Select physical activities to become part of your daily routine.
3. Search for podcasts and other ways to take your lessons on the go.
4. Don't forget to take breaks and stretch!

WELLNESS: MIND, BODY, AND SPIRIT HEALTH

Wellness means striking a healthy balance among the mind, body, and spirit that results in an overall feeling of well-being. The term has been defined by the Singapore-based National Wellness Association as an active process of becoming aware of and making choices toward a more successful existence.

DISEASE PREVENTION

You've heard it said that "an ounce of prevention is worth a pound of cure." So, let's think proactively. Wellness is more than the mere absence of disease; rather, it is an optimal state of health. The Harvard University School of Public Health created a series of calculators that assess your risk of developing cancer, heart disease, stroke, diabetes, and osteoporosis: You can find the calculators at http://www.yourdiseaserisk. com. After answering a series of questions, the site shows you your risk

8 ▶ REFLECTION QUESTIONS

- Is there anything about your lifestyle and/or family history that makes you at risk for a particular disease? Today, most diseases are not death sentences. How can you alter your lifestyle to best fight the disease?
- How would you rate your wellness in terms of disease prevention?

level and a customized action plan on how to alter it. Tips for diet, exercise, supplements, and lifestyle change are provided.

MENTAL HEALTH

Mental health refers to your emotional and psychological well-being. One way to think about mental health is by looking at how effectively and successfully a person functions. Feeling capable, competent, and independent, and being able to handle normal levels of stress, maintain satisfying relationships, and recover from difficult situations, are all signs of mental health.

Exercise and meditation are both proven ways to reduce the effect of stress on your mental health. Try to make time to shut off the computer and enjoy an hour of daylight. Scientists have found that the sun provides us with our main source of Vitamin D—a nutrient that strengthens our bones and muscles and boosts the immune system.

As an online student, especially if you work during the day, getting in your dose of daylight may prove tricky. Even a short walk has positive benefits. The sun can brighten your mood and even prevent depression. Your physical and mental well-being must function together to achieve overall health.

SLEEP

Balancing school, work, family, and other responsibilities may add up to sleep deprivation. For many busy adults, sleep is the element of a healthy lifestyle that most easily falls by the wayside. However, studies show that not getting enough sleep will cause problems in other aspects of your life.

Sleep deprivation results in a decrease in immune system function, problems with concentration, memory impairment, and poor performance at work and school. Sleep lays the groundwork for a productive day ahead.

There are only 24 hours in a day, and Chapter 7 provides some strategies for maximizing your time. Here are some strategies from the National Sleep Foundation for getting a good night's sleep:

▶ **Maintain a regular bedtime and wake time.** Our body has a clock that balances sleep and wake time. Regularity strengthens this function and can help you fall asleep at night.

▶ REFLECTION QUESTIONS

- How do you deal with stress?
- How do you deal with feelings of sadness?

Image copyright Anyka, 2009. Used under license from shutterstock.com

8

Image copyright Kharidehal Abhirama Ashwin, 2009. Used under license from shutterstock.com

8

- How would you rate your sleep habits? Do you regularly get a good night's sleep? Do you wake up in the morning feeling refreshed?
- If you rated your sleep habits as poor, how do you think you could improve upon them?

▶ **Relax before bed.** Avoid activities that can cause excitement, stress, or anxiety before bedtime. Listening to music with the lights off, taking a hot bath, and meditating are all ways to relax before bed.

▶ **Your bedroom should be for sleep only.** If possible, keep your computer, TV, and work outside of your bedroom. Your bedroom should be quiet, dark, and comfortable for sleeping.

▶ **Ensure that your mattress and pillows are comfortable.** Your mattress may have exceeded its life expectancy. Flipping it could buy some time. There are many types of mattresses and pillows on the market to accommodate various sleeping preferences. Choose one that is right for you.

▶ **Don't eat/drink caffeine before bedtime.** It is best to finish eating two to three hours before attempting to fall asleep. Heavy meals and spicy foods may make you less comfortable. Caffeine is a stimulant and can disrupt your sleep. Avoid caffeine within six to eight hours of going to bed.

▶ **Exercise regularly.** Regular exercise is the perfect antidote to sleepless nights. Aside from everything else you have learned in this chapter about exercise, it also promotes a sounder sleep. Try to finish your exercise at least three hours before bedtime.

AILMENTS TO AVOID

Over the past decade, research has shown that computer users are especially prone to repetitive strain injuries (RSI). RSI is a medically accepted condition that occurs when muscles, tendons, and nerves in the arms, neck, and back are kept tense for very long periods of time due to poor posture and/or repetitive motions. So in addition to maintaining proper nutrition, fitness, and sleep, online learners should look out for these "special" health issues. Although you may not encounter any of the ailments described next, awareness will help you spot warning symptoms and adjust your behavior accordingly.

Eyestrain

Eyestrain occurs when you overuse your eye muscles. Any muscle held in one position too long will strain. Working at the computer for a length of time can cause your eyes to get irritated, dry, and uncomfortable. Symptoms of eyestrain include sore, tired, itchy, watery, or dry eyes; blurred or double vision; headache and sore neck; and increased sensitivity to light.

Eyestrain associated with computer use isn't thought to have long-term consequences, but it is disruptive and unpleasant. The Mayo Clinic offers these tips to reduce and relieve eyestrain:

▶ **Take eye breaks.** Shift your focus away from the screen to something in the distance. Hold your eyes there for a few seconds and then shift back to your screen. Do "eye exercises" several times a day (see http://ergocise.com/eyes.html).

▶ **Change the pace.** Stand up, move around, and do work away from the computer. Even close your eyes for a few minutes.

▶ **Blink often to refresh your eyes.** Dry eyes can result from prolonged computer use. To lubricate your eyes, make a conscious effort to blink often.

▶ **Get appropriate eyewear.** Although high-index and anti-glare lenses cost more, the increase in price is worthwhile for computer users. Slight differences in the type of lens and coating can have a big impact on the comfort of your eyes.

▶ **Adjust your monitor.** Position your monitor directly in front of you about 20 to 28 inches from your eyes.

8

Carpal Tunnel Syndrome

Carpal Tunnel Syndrome (CTS) is a condition in which the median nerve (the nerve that runs down the forearm) is compressed at the wrist leading to pain and weakness in the forearm and hand.

Symptoms of CTS include numbness, burning, and tingling in the fingers. Difficulty in gripping and making a fist, dropping objects, and weakness may be signs that the condition is progressing.

The most effective way to prevent CTS is to take frequent breaks from repetitive movement such as computer keyboard usage. Voice recognition is a technology that has been improving over the years and can be a way to "talk-type" rather than "touch-type." A more passive move is to install software that reminds you to take breaks and stretch your hands and wrists. Stretch break freeware is available at http://www.workrave.com and http://ergocise.com/wrists.html.

Back and Neck Pain

Good posture is your best prevention for back and neck problems. Computer use coupled with bad posture can lead to back and neck pain, stiffness, and decreased range of motion.

Back and neck pain can be prevented by adopting an ergonomic workstation arrangement; doing stretching and strengthening exercises for the neck, back, and shoulders (see http://ergocise.com/neck.html

Image copyright Rod Ferris, 2009. Used under license from shutterstock.com

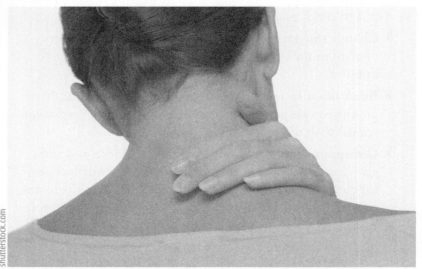

Image copyright Eric Gevaert, 2009. Used under license from shutterstock.com

8

and http://ergocise.com/back.html); taking regular breaks from the computer; and practicing proper posture at the computer.

success steps

TIPS FOR MAINTAINING YOUR WELL-BEING

1. Assess your risk levels for disease, and adjust your lifestyle for prevention.

2. Take care of your mental health.

3. Find activities to relieve stress, such as exercise or meditation.

4. Practice good sleep habits.

5. Maintain good posture and an ergonomic workstation to reduce your risk of repetitive strain injuries.

CHAPTER SUMMARY

Good health habits are the foundation for success in all of the areas discussed in *100% Online Student Success*. This chapter focused on the importance of nutrition, fitness, and wellness. The demands of your studies coupled with all of your other responsibilities require you to be of sound mind and body. To face the challenges ahead, fortify your foundation by choosing a healthy lifestyle.

POINTS TO KEEP IN MIND

In this chapter, several main points were discussed in detail:

▶ Nutrition and fitness are critical to good health, high energy, and the focus and attention needed to be a successful student.

▶ The USDA's MyPyramid serves as an excellent guide to good food choices.

▶ Timing your meals is important. Don't skip breakfast. Space your meals evenly throughout the day to sustain energy and reduce cravings.

▶ Water offers nothing but benefit to your body. Drink eight glasses a day.

▶ Exercise is essential to good health. With a little creativity, busy online students can add physical activity to their routines.

8

▶ Stretch breaks relieve tension, elongate muscles, and prevent repetitive strain injuries. Take them often!

▶ Sleep lays the groundwork for a productive day ahead. You can increase the quality of your sleep by practicing good sleep habits.

▶ Your physical and mental well-being must function together to achieve overall health.

LEARNING OBJECTIVES REVISITED

Review the learning objectives for this chapter, and rate your level of achievement for each objective using the rating scale provided. For each objective on which you do not rate yourself as a 3, outline a plan of action that you will take to fully achieve the objective. Include a time frame for this plan.

1 = did not successfully achieve objective

2 = understand what is needed, but need more study or practice

3 = achieved learning objective thoroughly

	1	2	3
Identify important components involved in achieving optimal health.	☐	☐	☐
Explain the dietary guidelines for Americans represented in the MyPyramid icon.	☐	☐	☐
Explain the differences between whole foods and processed foods.	☐	☐	☐
Explain the difference between good and bad cholesterol and between good and bad fat.	☐	☐	☐
List several reasons why breakfast is a crucial part of your diet.	☐	☐	☐
Explain the importance of water in your nutrition plan.	☐	☐	☐
Define *body mass index* (BMI).	☐	☐	☐
Describe creative ways to fit exercise into your busy schedule.	☐	☐	☐
Explain the importance of stretch breaks and which body parts to stretch.	☐	☐	☐
Describe how to set up an ergonomic workstation.	☐	☐	☐
Define *wellness* and how it relates to your overall health plan.	☐	☐	☐
Explain the importance of sleep, and identify strategies for getting a good night's sleep.	☐	☐	☐
Define *repetitive strain injury,* and identify symptoms and methods of prevention.	☐	☐	☐

8

Steps to Achieve Unmet Objectives

Steps   Due Date

1. _____   _____

2. _____   _____

3. _____   _____

4. _____   _____

5. _____   _____

6. _____   _____

7. _____   _____

REFERENCES

Carpal tunnel syndrome. Retrieved September 17, 2007, from http://www.ergocize.com

Grossman, M. Computer eye strain: How to relieve it. Retrieved from VisionWorks, Inc.: http://www.visionworksusa.com/computereyestrain.htm

Harvard School of Public Health. Fats and cholesterol: The good, the bad, and the healthy diet. Retrieved from http://www.hsph.harvard.edu/nutritionsource/fats.html

National Heart Lung and Blood Institute – Obesity Education Initiative. Controlling your weight. Retrieved from http://www.nhlbi.nih.gov/health/public/heart/obesity/lose_wt/control.htm

The National Sleep Foundation. Sleep tips: promoting a healthy sleep style. Retrieved from http://www.vcu.edu/sleepwell/pdfs/Sleep%20Tips.pdf

Readers Digest. The vitamins you need. Retrieved from http://health.ivillage.com/eating/enutritional/0,,rdigest_7hz7z2xs,00.html

United States Department of Agriculture. Steps to a healthier you. Retrieved from http://www.mypyramid.gov

8

CHAPTER OUTLINE

Improving Your Financial Health Through Online Education

Basic Practices of Financial Management

Budgeting 101

Budgeting for Online Education

Financial Resources for Online College

9 Financial Considerations

LEARNING OBJECTIVES

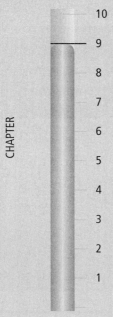

By the end of this chapter, students should have achieved the following objectives:

- ▶ Describe how education can impact your financial health.
- ▶ Be able to determine a budget for income and expenses.
- ▶ Explain the difference between *fixed* and *variable* income and expenses.
- ▶ Identify several ways you can save money with an online education.
- ▶ Define several forms of financial assistance and how they differ.
- ▶ Explain the difference between *subsidized* and *unsubsidized* loans.
- ▶ Describe how to find out about tuition reimbursement from your employer.

● TOPIC SCENARIO

Martha works full time at a national insurance company. She has been with the company since high school and has reached the salary ceiling for her position. Her mentor suggested she go back to school to earn a higher degree and apply for an opening in management. Martha knows that with her job, long commute, and family and community responsibilities, she would not have time to attend a traditional college. She also wonders how she will pay for her education. At the urging of her mentor, Martha has begun looking at online college degrees.

Based on Martha's situation, answer the following questions:

◗ How might Martha's employer be of assistance in her financial planning?

◗ What other avenues of financial aid might Martha be able to explore?

◗ In what ways could an online program fit into Martha's busy lifestyle?

◗ In what ways could an advanced degree help her get ahead in her career?

Image copyright fred goldstein, 2009. Used under license from shutterstock.com

9

❝ *Money is better than poverty, if only for financial reasons.*

—Woody Allen,
Oscar award-winning filmmaker

IMPROVING YOUR FINANCIAL HEALTH THROUGH ONLINE EDUCATION

What is the financial benefit of online learning? Many students would say it is the prospect of being prepared for a career that is personally and financially rewarding. This makes online learning a good investment. When you allocate money for developing skills that make you more employable, you are investing in your most important asset, yourself.

COST/BENEFIT ANALYSIS

In a competitive job market, those with the best professional, technical, and interpersonal skills will be the most attractive to employers. Successful online learners have the talent set that employers seek. That gives you, the successful online learner, an edge over other job candidates without the benefits of an online education.

The U.S. Department of Labor provides statistics that demonstrate the connection between level of education and earning power. The following chart illustrates how average salaries increase with degree completion.

	Weekly Earnings (Women - 2002)	Weekly Earnings (Men - 2002)
Less than high school diploma	$323.00	$421.00
High school graduate, no college	$459.00	$616.00
Associate degree or some college	$545.00	$732.00
College graduate	$809.00	$1,089.00

Source: U.S. Department of Labor. Earnings data in this article are annual average median usual weekly earnings of full-time wage and salary workers 25 years of age and older expressed in constant 2002 dollars.

9

Image copyright Szymon Apanowicz, 2009. Used under license from shutterstock.com

Men who dropped out of high school had earnings of $421 a week in 2002. Men who graduated from college saw their earnings rise 20% from $908 to $1,089. When adjusted for inflation, earnings for women with college degrees have increased by 33% from $605 to $809. At all levels of education, women have fared better than men with respect to earnings growth.

There is no doubt that higher education comes with a cost. Even with assistance from federal or state grant and loan programs, students must assume personal financial responsibility. While you are enrolled in an online learning program, you will need to understand the costs of your program and consider these as you prepare your budget.

REFLECTION QUESTIONS

- In what ways do you think higher education could help advance your career?
- What skills could you develop that could increase your income?

9

Apply **It!**

Cost Benefit Analysis: The DuVivier "Educational Value" Calculator

Goal: *Using your computer's calculator, determine the financial impact and value of your education (approximate values are okay).*

STEP 1: Key in the amount of yearly tuition for your online learning program.

$_____ (A, annual cost of online program)

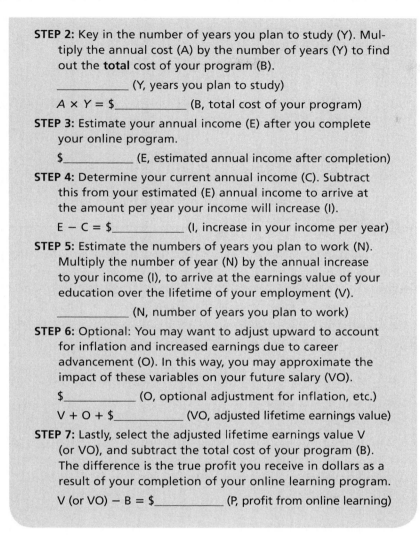

STEP 2: Key in the number of years you plan to study (Y). Multiply the annual cost (A) by the number of years (Y) to find out the **total** cost of your program (B).

_____ (Y, years you plan to study)

$A \times Y = \$$_____ (B, total cost of your program)

STEP 3: Estimate your annual income (E) after you complete your online program.

$\$$_____ (E, estimated annual income after completion)

STEP 4: Determine your current annual income (C). Subtract this from your estimated (E) annual income to arrive at the amount per year your income will increase (I).

$E - C = \$$_____ (I, increase in your income per year)

STEP 5: Estimate the numbers of years you plan to work (N). Multiply the number of year (N) by the annual increase to your income (I), to arrive at the earnings value of your education over the lifetime of your employment (V).

_____ (N, number of years you plan to work)

STEP 6: Optional: You may want to adjust upward to account for inflation and increased earnings due to career advancement (O). In this way, you may approximate the impact of these variables on your future salary (VO).

$\$$_____ (O, optional adjustment for inflation, etc.)

$V + O + \$$_____ (VO, adjusted lifetime earnings value)

STEP 7: Lastly, select the adjusted lifetime earnings value V (or VO), and subtract the total cost of your program (B). The difference is the true profit you receive in dollars as a result of your completion of your online learning program.

V (or VO) $- B = \$$_____ (P, profit from online learning)

BASIC PRACTICES OF FINANCIAL MANAGEMENT

As can be true with diet and exercise struggles, some people have an ingrained set of habits that keep them from reaching their financial goals. Taking control of your personal success involves coming to terms with money. No matter what your goals for the future may be, you'll need money to achieve them. Money dictates your purchasing

▶ REFLECTION QUESTIONS

- What techniques do you currently use to manage your finances?
- Do you have a budget?

power. You'll need to acquire the money you need and manage it well to get what you want.

You need to manage your financial resources just like you manage your time and your energy. With a money management plan in place, you'll be prepared to meet your financial goals. Remember, you do your best in activities where you can use your strengths and advantages. So, your approach to financial management should incorporate tried and true best practices in a way that works for you. That way, they can be readily sustained.

● BUDGETING 101

Basic budgeting involves reviewing your income and expenses and making decisions on how you use your money. The decisions you make affect how quickly or slowly you will meet your financial goals or if you will meet them at all. You need to have insight into where your money currently comes from, how often it arrives, and where it goes. This analysis gives you a picture of your current situation.

Now, let's dream about where you want to be. What financial position do you need to be in to do what you want to do? Ask yourself how your financial practices can be aligned to help you reach the goals you value most.

Establishing financial objectives and prioritizing your activities to reach those goals should happen next. The following tables show you the income and expense factors to consider developing a basic budget.

BASIC BUDGET WORKSHEET

Household Income

- My salary
- Other salary
- Variable employment (all)
- Alimony or child support (all)
- Government subsides (social security, Medicare, Medicaid)
- Income tax refund
- Interest on savings accounts
- Gifted monies

Household and Personal Expenses

- Home mortgage, home insurance, home equity line of credit, or rent
- Utilities (heat, electricity, water, and sewer)
- Television (cable/satellite), phone (land and/or cell), Internet access
- Transportation (gasoline, vehicle insurance, car payment, car repairs, parking)
- Food (groceries, restaurant meals)
- Household items, household repairs
- Personal shopping
- Medication and healthcare costs
- Education costs (tuition, books)

Go back over the two lists, and highlight the income and expenses you have that are fixed. This is the money earned or spent that does not vary each month.

Choose a different color to highlight the income and expenses you have that are varied. These are areas where you can exercise choice. Consider what activities you could add or change to increase your income and decrease your spending. Many people are in shock when they realize how much a daily cup of coffee or a cigarette habit adds up to at the end of the month.

▶ REFLECTION QUESTIONS

- What are some areas where you could improve or revise your spending patterns?
- Did your budget highlight any spending habits you could completely remove?

Image copyright Ingvald Kaldhussater, 2009. Used under license from shutterstock.com

9

Apply It!

Budgeting Basics

Goal: To select a financial management plan that fits your personality profile.

STEP 1: Visit the following Web sites:

- http://www.suzeorman.com
- http://www.moneycontrol.com
- http://www.smartmoney.com
- http://www.money.cnn.com
- http://www.bankrate.com
- http://www.fool.com

STEP 2: Read the different approaches to financial management. Consider all you know about your own personality. Think about which aspects of your personality will serve you well in financial planning and which will make it difficult.

STEP 3: After you review the approaches recommended by the financial gurus, select or develop a system that you feel will work best for you. Are there adjustments you will need to make in your natural style to increase your success?

STEP 4: (Optional) Review financial management software packages such as Quicken, QuickBooks, and Microsoft Money. You can also search Download.com for financial management freeware. It is important that you use a system that meets your needs, and the tools to support the system shouldn't break your bank.

BUDGETING FOR ONLINE EDUCATION

In addition to household and personal expenses, you will incur costs related directly to your online education. Some expenses, such as tuition, are fixed. However, the savvy student can take a thrifty approach to online studies. You may already have much of what you need, including your classroom (home) and computer.

ONLINE EDUCATION EXPENSES

▶ Tuition

▶ Books

▶ Computer

▶ Word-processing software

▶ Desk/chair/light

▶ Internet connection

Short on Funds?

▶ **Tuition.** See "Financial Resources for Online College" later in this chapter.

▶ **Books.** Check to see if the textbooks are available used at http://www.amazon.com or http://www.powells.com. You may also be able to save money (and trees) with e-books or PDFs.

▶ **Computer.** Used computers are a gamble and not always worth the savings when a virus or terminal error shows up a few months down the road. Comparison shop in electronics stores, look for deals online, and request a student discount.

▶ **Word-processing software.** eBay is a great place to get new, factory-sealed software at discount prices. Many manufacturers also give student discounts directly through their Web sites. Your computer may come with a basic word-processing package preloaded. To expand on it, Google offers a suite of word-processing applications (including spreadsheets and e-mail) hosted entirely on their servers (so no software to download, install, or maintain). The suite is free for educational use at http://www.google.com/a/edu.

▶ **Desk/chair/light.** Whereas used hardware and software is not recommended, go to town on your workstation, literally! Go to yard sales, thrift stores, and closeout sales, or check out http://www.craigslist.org. An ergonomic workstation need not cost a lot to be comfortable.

▶ **Internet connection.** There is so much competition for your business among the telecommunications providers that if you find out your neighbor is paying less than you, you can call your company and request a better deal. Beware of introductory

9

Image copyright VanHart, 2009. Used under license from shutterstock.com

REFLECTION QUESTIONS

- Do you already have some of the equipment and services you need to enroll in an online education program?
- What are some steps you can take to get the rest of what you need while adhering to your budget?

low rates that go up after three months. A dial-up Internet connection can be as low as $10 a month with DSL ranging from $19.99 to $50+ depending on your speed needs. See Chapter 3 for more about the types of Internet connections.

MAKING SAVING A HABIT

Any idea that is firmly implanted in our thinking causes us to act in a certain way. You can increase your financial assets by making a habit of saving something from each paycheck you receive. Check interest rates at lending institutions, and select the best place to put your money and watch it grow. Banks give varying interest on savings accounts; some banks give interest on checking accounts. If you can afford to park you money for at least six months, you can guarantee yourself a higher yield with a money market CD account. When saving money becomes a habit, you are on the road to improved financial security. Check out Bankrate.com or banks, savings and loans, credit unions, and other commercial lenders to compare best rates.

Remember, a strong commitment to attaining your goals will keep you armed to make sound financial decisions. First you must be aware of your spending, saving, and bill paying patterns. Next, be honest with yourself about where you can and should effect change. Finally, practice financial discipline until your habit of enhancing your goals becomes ingrained in your thoughts and actions.

Image copyright Mark Stout Photography, 2009. Used under license from shutterstock.com

THE PERILS OF DEBT

Debt is the enemy of habitual saving. Rather than getting ahead financially, debt can cause you to lose ground and fall behind. Whenever you take out a loan, put a clear plan in place to pay back the debt within a defined period of time. This should be the case whether the loan is for a car, a house, or your education.

Keep in mind that you not only will need to pay back the amount you borrowed, but lenders also charge interest for using their money. The amount of interest needs to be considered when you make the decision to borrow. If you are taking out a loan to further your education and eventually will allow you to earn more income, you may decide that the money you pay in interest is well worth it. On the other hand, if you purchase nonessential items with a credit card, the high interest rates may represent a financial mistake that moves you farther away from financial success.

9

FINANCIAL RESOURCES FOR ONLINE COLLEGE

Many resources are available to help pay for college, including personal savings, need-based financial aid, merit-based scholarships, federal loans and grants, work-study programs, and employer tuition

- How knowledgeable are you about financial aid resources? Where could you go to find out more information?
- Have you applied for all of the financial aid options available to you?

reimbursement. The type of funding varies based on individual situations, but it never hurts to apply.

FINANCIAL AID

Regardless of your current income level or need, you may qualify for a variety of student financial aid programs that can help offset your tuition costs.

▶ **Grants.** Based on need and do not have to be repaid.

▶ **Loans.** Based on need and other criteria. Federal loans are either subsidized (government pays the loan interest) or unsubsidized (borrower is responsible for the loan interest). Loan amounts vary, and repayment can be deferred until after graduation.

▶ **Scholarships.** Based on merit. They are available through the colleges, private individuals, and community groups, and usually do not have to be repaid.

▶ **Work-study programs.** Offer students the option to work while attending school and may be subsidized by the state or college.

Type of Aid	Examples	For More Information
Grants	• Pell grants	http://www.thepell.com
	• Federal Supplemental Educational Opportunity Grants	http://www.fseog.com http://www.ed.gov
Loans	• Government loans	http://www.staffordloan.com
	• Private lenders	http://esfweb.com
Scholarships	• Through the college	http://www.fastweb.com
	• Through individuals	http://www.freschinfo.com
Work-study	• Through the college	http://www.ed.gov
	• Government subsidized	http://www.ceiainc.org

success steps

COMPLETING FINANCIAL AID FORMS

1. Decide which types of financial aid you are eligible for.

2. Read all instructions, and review all forms.

3. Note important deadlines on your computer's calendar. Use the reminder feature if necessary.

4. Write or type legibly.

5. Review the completed form.

6. Keep copies for your reference.

EMPLOYER TUITION REIMBURSEMENT

You may be able to save thousands of dollars by asking your employer to pay for some of your education through a tuition reimbursement program. Employers understand that education is the key to success. Many large companies offer tuition reimbursement programs for employees who take courses related to their work. Some part-time jobs also offer limited tuition assistance. To qualify for tuition reimbursement, you usually have to have been employed at the company for a minimum amount of time.

Apply **It!**

Tuition Reimbursement

Goal: To find out if you qualify for tuition reimbursement.

STEP 1: Visit your human resources department Web site to learn more about whether your company offers tuition reimbursement.

STEP 2: Create a list of classes you want to take and the ways in which they would benefit the company. For instance:

- New skills
- Increased productivity
- Professional image

STEP 3: Anticipate your employer's possible concerns, and think of solutions. For example:

Concern: Your studies will take time away from work.

Solution: Online classes can be completed off the job and will give you skills to be more productive at work.

STEP 4: Set an appointment to discuss tuition reimbursement with your boss.

9

CREDIT FOR PRIOR LEARNING/EXPERIENCE

Many colleges recognize that adults and nontraditional students bring real-life experience to the classroom. This includes the knowledge and skills you have gained on the job. You may be able to earn credit for learning experiences that are the result of formal and informal work training, continuing education programs, self-instruction, and other sources. Your practical experiences can often be substituted for similar academic coursework, thereby reducing the amount of money you have to spend for your degree.

There is more than just financial incentive to learn on the job. The U.S. Department of Labor's Bureau of Labor Statistic's 2006–2007 report on Tomorrow's Jobs projected that 18.9 million jobs will be added to the U.S. economy by 2014. The report showed that 5 of the top 20 fastest growing jobs cite on-the-job training as the most significant source of postsecondary education.

While that's good news, it's important to note that a combination of higher education and on-the-job training is essential to finding your place in tomorrow's changing job market. The report also showed that on-the-job training is the most significant source of training for *all* 20 of the occupations with the largest numerical

Image copyright David Andrew Gilder, 2009. Used under license from shutterstock.com

9

decreases. These jobs—which include word processors, machine operators, and file clerks—will be partially or fully outmoded by advances in automation and technology.

CHAPTER SUMMARY

As the saying goes, you have to spend money to make money. Pursuing higher education, which develops your professional, technical, and interpersonal skills, is one of the smartest paths you can take for your personal and financial future. This chapter focused on the costs and benefits of online education. When you allocate money for developing skills that make you more employable, you are investing in your most important asset, yourself.

POINTS TO KEEP IN MIND

In this chapter, several main points were discussed in detail:

▶ The U.S. Department of Labor shows that increased education directly corresponds to greater earnings.

▶ Basic budgeting involves reviewing your income and expenses and making decisions on how you use your money.

▶ Consider habits you can change to increase your income and decrease your spending.

▶ You can increase your savings by putting away a little from each paycheck.

▶ Financial aid available for college includes grants, loans, scholarships, and work-study programs.

▶ Your employer may offer tuition reimbursement. You may also be eligible for college credit for skills you learned on the job.

LEARNING OBJECTIVES REVISITED

Review the learning objectives for this chapter, and rate your level of achievement for each objective using the rating scale provided. For each objective on which you do not rate yourself as a 3, outline a plan

9

of action that you will take to fully achieve the objective. Include a time frame for this plan.

1 = did not successfully achieve objective

2 = understand what is needed, but need more study or practice

3 = achieved learning objective thoroughly

	1	2	3
Describe how education can impact your financial health.	☐	☐	☐
Be able to determine a budget for income and expenses.	☐	☐	☐
Explain the difference between *fixed* and *variable* income and expenses.	☐	☐	☐
Identify several ways you can save money with an online education.	☐	☐	☐
Define several forms of financial assistance and how they differ.	☐	☐	☐
Explain the difference between *subsidized* and *unsubsidized* loans.	☐	☐	☐
Describe how to find out about tuition reimbursement from your employer.	☐	☐	☐

Steps to Achieve Unmet Objectives

Steps   Due Date

1. _____   _____

2. _____   _____

3. _____   _____

4. _____   _____

5. _____   _____

6. _____   _____

7. _____   _____

REFERENCES

Redenbach, S. Self-esteem and emotional intelligence, the necessary ingredients for success. Esteem Seminars Programs

Tracy, B. (2006). *Million dollar habits: Proven power practices to double and triple your income.* Entrepreneur Press.

U.S. Department of Labor. Retrieved from http://www.dol.gov/

Conclusion

MOVING ON FROM HERE

 And will you succeed?
Yes! You will indeed!
(98 and 3/4 percent guaranteed)

—Dr. Seuss
(Pulitzer Prize and Academy award-winning writer and cartoonist)

You are now familiar with the unique learning opportunities that online education presents. You understand that the skills you cultivate and develop as an online student provide the foundation for success in all aspects of your life. You should come away from *100% Online Student Success* with insight into your personality and learning style, ideas for community building, strategies for growth, and methods for achieving your educational goals.

Remember to keep these concepts in your mind so that you can readily apply them to your daily activities and any obstacles you encounter. Practice will make these techniques second nature to you. As you hone your communication and technology skills, you will become a more vital member of the ever-changing workforce. When you reach the end of your online program, the next books in the *100% Success* series, *100% Job Search Success* and *100% Career Success,* will support you in the continued development of your professional skills.

You have reached an effective introduction to the topics presented in *100% Online Student Success.* You are encouraged to use your Internet skills to seek out further knowledge and pursue your interests. Congratulations on your successes to date, and all the best to you as you pursue your goals.

Appendix A

THE APA STYLE: AN OVERVIEW

The American Psychological Association (APA) style is a widely accepted format for writing research papers, particularly for social science manuscripts and theses. The APA maintains standards for the layout of written documents, including the order of headings, formatting and organization of citations and references, and the arrangement of tables, figures, footnotes, and appendices. Entire books, guides, and Web sites are dedicated to explaining APA style. This appendix will briefly orient you to the APA style of citations. Remember, each source you cite in your paper must appear in your reference list; and each entry in the reference list must be properly cited in your text. You can obtain more information about specific citation issues and the APA style in the "Further Reading" section.

CITATIONS

Citations are references to outside sources within a passage of text. In APA style, a citation involves enclosing the author's last name and the date of publication within parentheses. The citations are generally placed immediately after the reference or at the end of the sentence in which the reference is made.

Basic Rules for APA-Style in-Text Citations

- Always capitalize proper nouns, including author names and initials.
- When capitalizing titles, capitalize both words in a hyphenated compound word and the first word after a dash or colon.

Capitalize all words that are four letters long or greater within the title of a source. Note that in your References list, only the first word of a title will be capitalized.

▶ Italicize or underline the titles of longer works such as books, edited collections, movies, television series, documentaries, or albums.

▶ Put quotation marks around the titles of shorter works such as journal articles, articles from edited collections, television series episodes, and song titles.

Examples of APA-Style Citations

Single Author

▶ A recent study confirmed the link between sleep deprivation and decreased test scores (Billinger, 2007).

▶ Billinger (2007) has confirmed that a lack of sleep immediately preceding a test, commonly known as cramming, results in decreased test scores.

Two Authors

▶ A recent study confirmed the link between sleep deprivation and decreased test scores (Billinger & Jacobs, 2007).

▶ Billinger and Jacobs (2007) have confirmed that a lack of sleep immediately preceding a test, commonly known as cramming, results in decreased test scores.

Three to Five Authors

▶ A recent study confirmed the link between sleep deprivation and decreased test scores (Billinger, Jacobs, & Janofsky, 2007).

▶ Billinger, Jacobs, and Janofsky (2007) have confirmed that a lack of sleep immediately preceding a test, commonly known as cramming, results in decreased test scores.

▶ Billinger et al. (2007) have confirmed that a lack of sleep immediately preceding a test, commonly known as cramming, results in decreased test scores.

▶ A recent study confirmed the link between sleep deprivation and decreased test scores (Billinger et al., 2007).

Six or More Authors

▶ Billinger et al. (2007) confirmed the link between sleep deprivation and decreased test scores.

Multiple Publications, Same Author

▶ A recent study confirmed the link between sleep deprivation and decreased test scores (Billinger, 2006, 2007a, 2007b).

▶ Billinger (2006, 2007a, 2007b) confirmed the link between sleep deprivation and decreased test scores.

Multiple Publications, Different Authors

▶ A recent study confirmed the link between sleep deprivation and decreased test scores (Altman, 2003; Billinger, 2006, 2007; Liles, 2005).

REFERENCES

Full bibliographic information should be provided in a References section at the end of the paper. APA style requires that the References section include only articles that are cited within the body of the text, as opposed to sources that have been used by the authors as background but not referred to or included in the body of a document.

Examples of APA-Style References

Book by One Author

Richardson, J. (2006). *Ahead of the pack: Balancing your way to personal success in college.* Clifton Park, NY: Thomson Delmar Learning.

Book by Two or More Authors

Solomon, A., Tyler, L., & Taylor, T. (2007). *100% job search success.* Clifton Park, NY: Thomson Delmar Learning.

Article in an Edited Book

Kibler, L., & Vannoy Kibler, P. (1998). When students resort to cheating. In R. Holkeboer (Ed.), *College Success Reader.* Boston: Houghton Mifflin.

Article in a Monthly Magazine

Henry, W. A., III. (1990, April 9). Making the grade in today's schools. *Time*, 135, 28–31.

Article in a Newspaper

Schultz, S. (2005, December 28). Calls made to strengthen state energy policies. *The Country Today*, pp. 1A, 2A.

Government Document

United States Department of Justice. (2004). A guide to disability rights laws.

Internet Article Based on a Print Source

Marlowe, P., Spade, S., & Chan, C. (2001). Detective work and the benefits of colour versus black and white [Electronic version]. *Journal of Pointless Research*, 11, 123–124.

Standalone Internet Document, No Author Identified, No Date

Middlebury College, Office of Learning Resources. (n.d.) *Study Skills*. Retrieved September 28, 2005, from http://www.middlebury.edu/academics/tools/olr/study_skills

A Page on a Web Site

Student financial aid. (2007, August 30). In Wikipedia, The Free Encyclopedia. Retrieved 03:28, September 17, 2007, from http://en.wikipedia.org/w/index.php?title=Student_financial_aid&oldid=154623991

Document Available on University Program or Department Web Site

Pelley, J. W. (2002). The success types learning style indicator: Introduction to your psychological type [Electronic Version]. Texas Tech University Health Sciences Center. Retrieved February 28, 2005, from http://www.ttuhsc.edu/SOM/Success/LSTIntro.htm

Basic Rules for the APA Style Reference List

▶ Your reference list should appear at the end of your paper on a new page separate from the text of the essay.

◗ All lines after the first line of each entry in your reference list should be indented one-half inch from the left margin.

◗ Authors' names are inverted: last name and then initials.

◗ Reference list entries should be alphabetized by the last name of the first author of each work.

FURTHER READING

By adopting and using an editorial format, such as the APA style, you help readers of your papers navigate and access material more efficiently. To learn more about APA style, read:

◗ *Publication Manual of the American Psychological Association* (5th ed.)

◗ *Mastering APA Style: Student's Workbook and Training Guide*

Internet Resources include the following:

◗ The APA Web site (http://apastyle.apa.org/)

◗ Sample APA research paper from Diana Hacker (http://www. dianahacker.com/pdfs/Hacker-Shaw-APA.pdf)

◗ Online APA documentation from a reputable college such as Purdue University's Online Writing Lab (http://owl.english. purdue.edu)

◗ Your online learning program's Web site or style guide

Appendix B

THE MLA STYLE: AN OVERVIEW

The *MLA Style Manual,* published by the Modern Language Association, is a style guide widely used in academia for writing and documentation of research in humanities and literature. According to its mission statement, the MLA aims to "strengthen the study and teaching of language and literature." As with the APA, there are entire books, guides, and Web sites dedicated to explaining the MLA style. This appendix will briefly orient you to the MLA style of citations. Remember, each source you cite in your paper must appear in your Works Cited list; and each entry in the Works Cited list must be properly cited in your text. You can obtain more information about specific citation issues and the MLA style in the "Further Reading" section.

CITATIONS

Citations are references to outside sources within a passage of text. In MLA style, a citation involves enclosing the author's last name and a page reference within parentheses. These citations are placed where a natural pause would occur, preferably at the end of a sentence.

Basic Rules for MLA-Style Citations

- Be concise. Usually the author's last name and a page reference are all that is needed.
- Citations should complement, not repeat, information that is given in your text.
- The citation should precede the punctuation mark that concludes the sentence, clause, or phrase that contains the cited material.

▶ When citing a work within the text of a paper, try to mention the material being cited in a "signal phrase" that includes the author's name. After that phrase, insert a citation, including the page number of the work from which the information is drawn.

▶ If the author is not mentioned in a "signal phrase," the author's name, followed by the page number, must appear in parentheses.

▶ If you are citing an entire work, or one without page numbers (or only one page), write just the author's name in parentheses.

Examples of MLA-Style Citations

Single Author

▶ Billinger has confirmed that a lack of sleep immediately preceding a test, commonly known as cramming, results in decreased test scores (37–43).

▶ A recent study confirmed the link between sleep deprivation and decreased test scores (Billinger, 37–43).

Two Authors

▶ Billinger and Jacobs (37–43) have confirmed that a lack of sleep immediately preceding a test, commonly known as cramming, results in decreased test scores.

▶ A recent study (Billinger & Jacobs, 2007) confirmed the link between sleep deprivation and decreased test scores.

Multiple Authors, Different Works

▶ This theory (Billinger, 69) is supported by prior studies on college students and sleep deprivation (Liles and Evje, 77–85).

Multiple Pages, Same Author

▶ Billinger discusses the effect of caffeine and other stimulants on students' test performance (18–21, 57).

Corporate Authors

▶ In a study commissioned by the President's Council on Physical Fitness and Sports, it was recommended that Americans get thirty minutes of aerobic exercise a day (17–25).

▸ Studies show that thirty minutes of aerobic exercise daily is optimal for most Americans (President's Council on Physical Fitness and Sports, 17–25).

Multivolume Works

▸ In Volume 3, Chong reports on the effects of chronic sleep reduction on the performance of cognitive tasks (173–201).

▸ Studies show a drastic reduction in the performance of cognitive tasks relative to chronic sleep reduction (Chong 3: 173–201).

Works with No Author

▸ As stated by the Presidential Commission (Report 3) . . .

▸ In a study by the American Academy of Family Physicians . . .

Works Cited

References cited in the text of a research paper must appear at the end of the paper in a Works Cited list or bibliography. This list provides the information necessary to identify and retrieve each source that supports your research. Note that the MLA heavily abbreviates publication information. If the work is not particularly well known, however, the author is advised to add publication details to help identify the source.

Examples of MLA-Style Works Cited

Book by One Author

Richardson, Josh. *Ahead of the Pack: Balancing Your Way To Personal Success In College.* Clifton Park: Thomson Delmar Learning, 2006.

Book by Two Authors

Gillespie, Paula, and Neal Lerner. *The Allyn and Bacon Guide to Peer Tutoring.* Boston: Allyn, 2000.

Book by Three or More Authors

Solomon, Amy, et al. *100% Job Search Success.* Clifton Park, NY: Thomson Delmar Learning, 2007.

Article in a Magazine

Henry, W. A., III. "Making the Grade in Today's Schools." <u>Time</u> 9 April 1990: 28–31.

Article in a Newspaper

Krugman, Andrew. "Fear of Eating." <u>New York Times</u> 21 May 2007 late ed.: A1.

Government Document

United States Department of Justice. <u>A Guide to Disability Rights Laws.</u> 2004.

An Entire Web Site

<u>The Purdue OWL Family of Sites.</u> 26 Aug. 2005. The Writing Lab and OWL at Purdue and Purdue University. 17 Sep 2007 http://owl.english.purdue.edu.

A Page on a Web Site

"Student financial aid." Wikipedia, The Free Encyclopedia. 30 Aug 2007, 16:36 UTC. Wikimedia Foundation, Inc. 17 Sep 2007 http://en.wikipedia.org/w/index.php?title=Student_financial_aid&oldid=154623991.

An Image

Goya, Francisco. The Family of Charles IV. 1800. Museo del Prado, Madrid. 17 Sep 2007 http://museoprado.mcu.es/i64a.html.

Basic Rules for MLA-Style Works Cited

▶ The Works Cited page should be centered and headed "Works Cited."

▶ All lines after the first line of each entry in your reference list should be indented one-half inch from the left margin.

▶ Entries should be alphabetized by authors' last names and double-spaced.

▶ Dates should be written with the day of the month first, the three letter abbreviation of the month, and the year (example: 1 Jan. 2000).

- Titles can either be underlined or italicized.

- Use the conjunction "and," not an ampersand (&), when listing multiple authors of a single work.

- Do not use the abbreviations p. or pp. to designate page numbers.

FURTHER READING

By adopting and using an editorial format, such as the MLA style, you help readers of your papers navigate and access material more efficiently. There are two official publications of the MLA presenting MLA style:

- The *MLA Style Manual and Guide to Scholarly Publishing* (2nd ed.) is addressed primarily to academic scholars, professors, graduate students, and other advanced-level writers of scholarly books and articles.

- The *MLA Handbook for Writers of Research Papers* (6th ed.) is addressed primarily to secondary school and undergraduate college and university students.

Internet resources include the following:

- The MLA Web site (http://www.mla.org)

- Sample MLA research paper from Diana Hacker (http://www.bedfordstmartins.com/hacker/pdf/mla.pdf)

- Online MLA documentation from a reputable college such as Purdue University's Online Writing Lab (http://owl.english.purdue.edu)

- Your online learning program's Web site or style guide

Index